THE BEST OF

SPITBALL

"For many of us the eternal question 'Is baseball a sport or a business?' is irrelevant. Baseball is a mania, an obsession, a joyful spending of hours, days, lives devoted to watching, second-guessing, discussing, arguing, analyzing favorite teams, players, games, strategies, moments. . . . The founders of *Spitball* magazine, Mike Shannon and the late Jim Harrison, had an idea—that there were writers in America like themselves, poets, short-story writers, and artists who wanted to say something about their passion, baseball. . . . As you read, skipping from piece to piece, listen for the passion. It's there on every page, along with the joy that only reading about baseball can bring."

—PETER GOLENBOCK,
from the Preface

"I enjoyed reading *The Best of Spitball*. The writers seem to have a deep affection for baseball and their stories reflect that emotion. . . . Mike Shannon's quixotic venture in publishing baseball's new fiction deserves acclaim. He hereby gets it from me."

—JIM BROSNAN,
author of *The Long Season* and *Pennant*

"Whenever I need to be reminded of the music of baseball, I read *Spitball*—its best pieces are as true as a shot to the wall."

—DANIEL OKRENT,
editor of *The Ultimate Baseball Book*

The Best of SPITBALL

The Literary Baseball Magazine

EDITED BY MIKE SHANNON

ILLUSTRATED, WITH A PREFACE
BY PETER GOLENBOCK

POCKET BOOKS
New York   London   Toronto   Sydney   Tokyo

An *Original* publication of POCKET BOOKS

POCKET BOOKS, a division of Simon & Schuster, Inc.,
1230 Avenue of the Americas, New York, N.Y. 10020

ISBN: 0-671-64983-3

First Pocket Books trade paperback printing March, 1988

10 9 8 7 6 5 4 3 2 1

PREFACE

by Peter Golenbock

Baseball, like religion, politics, and sex, is an enduring institution that has provided American society with a special, unique outlet for its passions. For many of us the eternal question "Is baseball a sport or a business?" is irrelevant. Whatever label one attaches to it, what it inevitably becomes is a mania, an obsession, a joyful spending of hours, days, lives devoted to watching, second-guessing, discussing, arguing, analyzing favorite teams, players, games, strategies, moments.

When I was growing up the Presidential choices were "Ike or Stevenson?" "Kennedy or Nixon?" But more important, "Mantle, Mays, or Snider?" "Williams or Musial?" And unlike the temporal Presidential debates, "Mantle, Mays, or Snider" and "Williams or Musial" have become eternal questions. My friends, in their forties, still argue their positions. As they will when they are in their eighties, with the same youthful enthusiasm as the kids today debate "Don Mattingly or Keith Hernandez?" "Ozzie Smith or God?"

No tie binds this country like Baseball. Black, white, Christian, Jew, Hindu, Moslem, gay or straight,

5

pro-abortion, pro-life, the disparate interest groups agree on little except for their love of the National Pastime. Go to a ball game. In Fenway Park Harvard professors sit and talk the same language with the fans with blue collars. All agree: Jim Rice never hits in the clutch.

The uninitiated are always overwhelmed by the lengths Baseball devotees will go to in order to follow their passions. To me it is quite normal. And healthy. Of my friends and acquaintances who spend their lives in their search for Diamond Truths or Diamond Stars, I can think of none who are alcoholics or drug addicts and only one who has been divorced. These are men in their forties and fifties, happily married with children who often see their fathers as a little odd but who otherwise indulge Dad as he rummages through tag sales looking for 1955 Bowmans or as he watches reruns of the Mets–Astros playoff games on his VCR. Like G.E., Baseball apparently brings good things to life.

I'll never forget the day my friend Barry brought home a life-size wax figure of Babe Ruth. It was from Madame Tussaud's museum in London. Every few years the museum changes exhibits, and I guess Pete Rose was in and the Babe was out. Figuratively. So Barry bought the waxen Babe for his New Jersey den.

He had already acquired Babe Ruth's coat, hat, glove, his jock, and a lock of his hair. One day I expect to find the Babe himself buried in Barry's backyard. I suspect that dear departed Clair couldn't have loved the Babe as much as Barry does.

I know another Baseball Crazy named George who applied for and received from the great State of New York the vanity license plate BASEBALL and who when asked several years ago by Commissioner Bowie Kuhn for the plate "for the good of the game" stood firm. George hadn't forgiven Kuhn for disallowing the sale of Vida Blue to the Yankees. He also didn't want to give up the joy of having strangers stop him at lights and ask him how he thought the Mets were doing.

It is men's (and women's) passion for this sport that fascinates me. It appears in so many different forms. The Society of American Baseball Research (SABR) has grown into a powerful body with thousands of members who on their own, for the pure love and joy of it, research what might appear to be arcana and minutiae, the Negro Leagues, the Minor Leagues, the Mexican Leagues, old ballparks, and players who toiled before the turn of the century, the way archeologists once studied the Dead Sea scrolls. Does anyone really care that Ty Cobb was robbed of a base hit by a scoring error in 1908? These people do, and because they do, Baseball is richer for it and so are they.

Scratch the emotional surface of any baseball fan at any ballpark across America and you will find this deep-rooted multifaceted passion, in one form or another. Some fans continue to root for teams that no longer exist. There is a St. Louis Browns Fan Club that still meets. They have luncheons with the likes of Al Zarilla and Ned Garver. Some fans spend their lives rooting against one team (usually the Yankees). Some fans have a passion for one particular player (Ted Williams could still win the mayoral race in Boston). Some fans are interested only in the statistical aspects of the Game. Could *Poor Richard's Almanac* have been more important to colonial America than the annual Bill James

Baseball Abstract is to Sabermetric America today? No
way, Jose Cruz.

And then there are those, including Mr. James, who
spend their lives writing about the Game. I'm one of
them. I have spent the last fifteen years of my life writing
about Baseball. It has allowed me to travel around the
country interviewing baseball players and to meet and
become friends with talented Baseball junkies, writers
like Roger Kahn, Pat Jordon, and Ed Linn, and admiring
the devotion of others such as the founders of *Spitball*
magazine, Mike Shannon and the late Jim Harrison.
They had an idea—that there were writers in America
like themselves, poets, short-story writers, and artists
who wanted to say something about their passion, Base-
ball, but who had no outlet for their work. They decided
to provide that outlet. They financed it on a shoestring
and lovingly they nurtured it. Eight years later, *Spitball*
magazine is going strong. As you will see from reading
the diverse selections, *Spitball* has given unknown and
known writers and artists a chance for discovery, exper-
imentation, and growth. As you read, skipping from
piece to piece, listen for the passion. It's there on every
page, along with the joy that only reading about Baseball
can bring.

CONTENTS

9

EDITOR'S INTRODUCTION

Jim Harrison and I founded *Spitball* in the fall of 1980 over a handshake and a few beers in his turn-of-the-century rowhouse apartment in Covington, Kentucky, just two blocks and the Roebling suspension bridge south of Riverfront Stadium, the home of the Cincinnati Reds. We started *Spitball* because we strongly suspected that there were many poets and short-story writers "out there" writing about baseball with no place in particular to send their work. We wanted to provide such a place, to be, not a magazine where the editors might not disqualify a poem or a story because it was about baseball, but the magazine where use of baseball as subject matter was the first consideration.

Though many people reacted to our idea of a magazine combining literature and baseball with incomprehension or skepticism—*Writer's Digest* introduced us to its readers with "A new magazine of poetry exclusively on the subject of baseball? That's what they say"—nobody tried to stop us, and we published the first issue of *Spitball* in the spring of 1981. Today, that first issue, containing 13 poems and a total of 20 pages, looks like a rather slim and crude effort, but it was nevertheless, like a leadoff double, a good beginning. (The poems by Roland Flint and W. J. Harrison in this volume both appeared in No. 1.)

Almost everybody who read the first issue liked it— at least that's what they said—and submissions and subscriptions soon started coming in from all parts of the country. We really knew that we were on to something, however, when we received our first submission of 13 poems, nearly all of them excellent, from Gene Fehler, then of Alabama, now of Texas, before the publication of the second issue. Then in time for No. 3 we received two outstanding short stories that completely convinced us of *Spitball*'s purposefulness: "The Dome and the Hall of Famer" by Fehler and a marvelous piece of characterization and irony called "Old-Timers" by Jim Palana of Rockland, Massachusetts.

As with almost any new magazine, *Spitball* has undergone small changes in its formative years to evolve into what it is today. We didn't review books, for instance, until No. 4, and it wasn't until 1983 that we instituted the Casey Award (for best baseball book of the year) and began the practice of reviewing every new baseball book published. Once we realized that "Editors' Scorecard" sounded too similar to the name already in use by *Sports Illustrated,* we dropped it (with No. 8) for "Parnassian Pressbox," a much more appropriate name for *Spitball* anyway. Our wonderful Napoleon Lajoie logo (Lajoie holding, not a bat, but a quill pen) didn't appear until No. 9, and it wasn't until No. 16 (Winter 1985) that we began to display our subtitle, "The Literary Baseball Magazine," on the cover.

Through all the changes, though, one thing has remained constant: our excitement at bringing into print in every issue terrific new baseball poems and short stories, both by famous writers—the publication of W. P. Kinsella's "How I Got My Nickname" in No. 8 was an important *Spitball* milestone—and by the "unheralded but talented" variety. "Alibi Ike" (by Ring Lardner) and "You Could Look It Up" (by Thurber) are undisputed classics, but you won't find either in this book. (Even were this anthology not limited to writing which has appeared in *Spitball*, there would be at this juncture little point in reprinting them since they are available from half a dozen sources already.) What you will find here is a rich collection of fresh and original baseball stories and poems and trenchant interviews with great baseball writers which are available nowhere else—some of which, thanks to Pocket Books, can now take their rightful places among the other greats in anyone's lineup of favorite literary baseball writings.

Finally, *Spitball* has been blessed with too many friends for me to mention each one here individually, and I trust they know how much I appreciate their interest and support. Special thanks, however, must be given to the writers and artists who allowed us to reprint their works in this anthology, to all the other writers and artists who have contributed to *Spitball,* and to the past and present members of the *Spitball* art and editorial staffs: Blair Gibeau, Darryl Lankford, Annie Weghorn, Larry Dickson, Charles Virgil Smith, and Kevin Grace. I am especially grateful to three wonderful people whose generosity has made the publishing of *Spitball* not only possible but joyful: my former partner, now deceased,

W. J. (Jim) Harrison, his widow Pat Moore Harrison, and my own wife, Kathleen Dermody Shannon; and to Paul McCarthy cf Pocket Books who originated the idea of this anthology and saw it into being. But enough dugout chatter. It's time to step into the box and face some *Spitball* pitching!

Mike Shannon
October 1987

Spitball:

6224 Collegevue Pl.
Cincinnati, OH 45224

The Best of

SPITBALL

The
Literary Baseball
Magazine

W. P. KINSELLA

HOW I GOT MY NICKNAME

*(For Brian Fawcett, whose story
"My Career with the Leafs" inspired this.)*

In the summer of 1951, the summer before I was to start
Grade 12, my polled Hereford calf, Simon Bolivar, won
Reserve Grand Champion at the Des Moines, All-Iowa
Cattle Show and Summer Exposition. My family lived
on a hobby-farm near Iowa City. My father, who taught
classics at Coe college in Cedar Rapids, and in spite of
that was still the world's number-one baseball fan, said I
deserved a reward—I also had a straight A average in
Grade 11 and had published my first short story that
spring. My father phoned his friend Robert Fitzgerald
(Fitzgerald, an eminent translator, sometimes phoned
my father late at night and they talked about various
ways of interpreting the tougher parts of *The Iliad*) and
two weeks later I found myself in Fitzgerald's spacious
country home outside of New York City, sharing the
lovely old house with the Fitzgerald's, their endless
supply of children, and a young writer from Georgia

named Flannery O'Connor. Miss O'Connor was charming, and humorous in an understated way, and I wish I had talked with her more. About the third day I was there I admitted to being a published writer and Miss O'Connor said, "You must show me some of your stories." I never did. I was seventeen, overweight, diabetic, and bad-complexioned. I alternated between being terribly shy and obnoxiously brazen. I was nearly always shy around the Fitzgeralds and Miss O'Connor. I was also terribly homesick, which made me appear more silent and outlandish than I knew I was. I suspect I am the model for Enoch Emery, the odd, lonely countryboy in Miss O'Connor's novel *Wise Blood*. But that is another story.

On a muggy August morning, the first day of a Giants home stand at the Polo Grounds, I prepared to travel into New York. I politely invited Miss O'Connor to accompany me, but she, even at that early date, had to avoid sunlight and often wore her wide-brimmed straw hat, even indoors. I set off much too early and, though terrified of the grimy city and shadows that seemed to lurk in every doorway, arrived at the Polo Grounds over two hours before game time. It was raining gently and I was one of about two dozen fans in the ballpark. A few players were lethargically playing catch, a coach was hitting fungoes to three players in right field. I kept edging my way down the rows of seats until I was right behind the Giants dugout.

The Giants were thirteen games behind the Dodgers and the pennant race appeared all but over. A weasel-faced bat boy, probably some executive's nephew, I thought, noticed me staring wide-eyed at the players and the playing field. He curled his lip at me, then stuck out his tongue. He mouthed the words "Take a picture, it'll last longer," adding something at the end that I could only assume to be uncomplimentary.

Fired by the insult I suddenly mustered all my bravado and called out, "Hey, Mr. Durocher!" Leo Durocher, the Giants manager, had been standing in the third-base coach's box not looking at anything in particular. I was really impressed. That's the grand thing about baseball, I thought. Even a manager in a pennant race can take time to daydream. He didn't hear me, but the bat boy did and stuck out his tongue again.

I was overpowered by my surroundings. Though I'd seen a lot of major league baseball, I'd never been in the Polo Grounds before. The history of the place . . . "Hey, Mr. Durocher," I shouted.

Leo looked up at me with a baleful eye. He needed a shave, and the lines around the corners of his mouth looked like ruts.

"What is it, kid?"

"Could I hit a few?" I asked hopefully, as if I were begging to stay up an extra half hour. "You know, take a little batting practice?"

"Sure, kid. Why not?" and Leo smiled with one corner of his mouth. "We want all our fans to feel like part of the team."

From the box seat where I'd been standing, I climbed up on the roof of the dugout and Leo helped me down onto the field.

Leo looked down into the dugout. The rain was stopping. On the other side of the park a few of the Phillies were wandering onto the field. "Hey, George," said Leo, staring into the dugout, "throw the kid here a few pitches. Where you from, son?"

It took me a minute to answer because I experienced this strange light-headed feeling, as if I had had too much sun. "Near to Iowa City, Iowa," I managed to say in a small voice. Then, "You're going to win the pennant, Mr. Durocher. I just know you are."

"Well, thanks, kid," said Leo modestly, "we'll give it our best shot."

George was George Bamberger, a stocky rookie who had seen limited action. "Bring the kid a bat, Andy," Leo said to the bat boy. The bat boy curled his lip at me but slumped into the dugout, as Bamberger and Sal Yvars tossed the ball back and forth.

The bat boy brought me a black bat. I was totally unprepared for how heavy it was. I lugged it to the plate and stepped into the right-hand batter's box. Bamberger delivered an easy, looping, batting-practice pitch. I drilled it back up the middle.

"Pretty good, kid," I heard Leo say.

Bamberger threw another easy one and I fouled it off. The third pitch was a little harder. I hammered it to left.

"Curve him," said Durocher.

He curved me. Even through my thick glasses the ball looked as big as a grapefruit, illuminated like a small moon. I whacked it and it hit the right-field wall on one bounce.

"You weren't supposed to hit that one," said Sal Yvars.

"You're pretty good, kid," shouted Durocher from the third-base box. "Give him your best stuff, George."

Over the next fifteen minutes I batted about .400

against George Bamberger and Roger Bowman, including a home run into the left centerfield stands. The players on the Giants bench were watching me with mild interest, often looking up from the books most of them were reading.

"I'm gonna put the infield out now," said Durocher. "I want you to run out some of your hits."

Boy, here I was batting against the real New York Giants. I wished I'd worn a new shirt instead of the horizontally striped red and white one I had on, which made me look heftier than I really was. Bowman threw a sidearm curve and I almost broke my back swinging at it. But he made the mistake of coming right back with the same pitch. I looped it behind third where it landed soft as a sponge, and trickled off toward the stands—I'd seen the play hundreds of times—a stand-up double. But when I was still twenty feet from second base, Eddie Stanky was waiting with the ball. "Slide!" somebody yelled, but I just skidded to a stop, stepping out of the baseline to avoid the tag. Stanky whapped me anyway, a glove to the ribs that would have made Rocky Marciano or Ezzard Charles proud.

When I got my wind back, Durocher was standing, hands on hips, staring down at me.

"Why the hell didn't you slide, kid?"

"I can't," I said, a little indignantly. "I'm diabetic. I have to avoid stuff like that. If I cut myself, or even bruise badly, it takes forever to heal."

"Oh," said Durocher. "Well, I guess that's okay then."

"You shouldn't tag people so hard," I said to Stanky. "Somebody could get hurt."

"Sorry, kid," said Stanky. I don't think he apologized very often. I noticed that his spikes were filed. But I found later that he knew a lot about F. Scott Fitzgerald. His favorite story was "Babylon Revisited," so that gave us a lot in common; I was a real Fitzgerald fan; Stanky and I became friends even though both he and Durocher argued against reading *The Great Gatsby* as an allegory.

"Where'd you learn your baseball?" an overweight coach who smelled strongly of snuff and bourbon said to me.

"I live near Iowa City, Iowa," I said in reply.

Everyone wore question marks on their faces. I saw I'd have to elaborate. "Iowa City is within driving distance of Chicago, St. Louis, Milwaukee, and there's minor league ball in Cedar Rapids, Omaha, Kansas City. Why there's barely a weekend my dad and I don't go somewhere to watch professional baseball."

"Watch?" said Durocher.

"Well, we talk about it some too. My father is a real student of the game. Of course we only talk in Latin when we're on the road, it's a family custom."

"Latin?" said Durocher.

"Say something in Latin," said Whitey Lockman, who had wandered over from first base.

"The Etruscans have invaded Gaul," I said in Latin.

"Their fortress is on the banks of the river," said Bill Rigney, who had been filling in at third base.

"*Velle est posse,*" I said.

"Where there's a will there's a way," translated Durocher.

"Drink Agri Cola . . ." I began.

"The farmer's drink," said Sal Yvars, slapping me on the back, but gently enough not to bruise me. I guess I looked a little surprised.

"Most of us are more than ballplayers," said Alvin Dark, who had joined us. "In fact, the average player on this squad is fluent in three languages."

"Watch?" said Durocher, getting us back to baseball. "You watch a lot of baseball, but where do you play?"

"I've never played in my life," I replied. "But I have a photographic memory. I just watch how different players hold their bats, how they stand. I try to emulate Enos Slaughter and Joe DiMaggio."

"Can you field?" said Durocher.

"No."

"No?"

"I've always just watched the hitters. I've never paid much attention to the fielders."

He stared at me as if I had spoken to him in an unfamiliar language.

"Everybody fields," he said. "What position do you play?"

"I've never played," I reiterated. "My health is not very good."

"Cripes," he said, addressing the sky. "You drop a second Ted Williams on me and he tells me he can't field." Then to Alvin Dark: "Hey, Darky, throw a few with the kid here. Get him warmed up."

In the dugout Durocher pulled a thin, black glove from an equipment bag and tossed it to me. I dropped it. The glove had no discernible padding in it. The balls Dark threw hit directly on my hand when I caught them, which was about one out of three. "Ouch!" I cried. "Don't throw so hard."

"Sorry, kid," said Alvin Dark. He threw the next one a little easier. If I really heaved, I could just get the ball back to him. I have always thrown like a nonathletic girl. I could feel my hand bloating inside the thin glove. After about ten pitches, I pulled my hand out. It looked as though it had been scalded.

"Don't go away, kid," said Leo. "In fact, why don't you sit in the dugout with me. What's your name anyway?"

"W. P. Kinsella," I said.

"Your friends call you W?"

"My father calls me William, and my mother . . ." but I let my voice trail off. I didn't think Leo Durocher would want to know my mother still called me Bunny.

"Jeez," said Durocher. "You need a nickname, kid. Bad."

"I'll work on it," I said.

I sat right beside Leo Durocher all that stifling afternoon in the Polo Grounds as the Giants swept a doubleheader from the Phils, the start of a sixteen-game streak that was to lead to the October 3, 1951, Miracle of Coogan's Bluff. I noticed right away that the Giants were all avid readers. In fact, the *New York Times* best-sellers lists, and the *Time* and *Newsweek* lists of readable books, and an occasional review were taped to the walls of the dugout. When the Giants were in the field, I peeked at the covers of the books the players sometimes read between innings. Willie Mays was reading *The Cruel Sea* by Nicholas Monsarrat. Between innings Sal Maglie was deeply involved in Carson McCuller's new novel *The Ballard of the Sad Cafe*. "I sure wish we could get that Cousin Lyman to be our mascot," he said to me when he saw me eyeing the book jacket, referring to the hunchbacked dwarf who was the main character in the novel. "We need something to inspire us," he added. Alvin Dark slammed down his copy of *Requieum for a Nun* and headed for the on-deck circle.

When the second game ended, a sweaty and sagging Leo Durocher took me by the arm. "There's somebody I want you to meet, kid," he said. Horace Stoneham's office was furnished in wine-colored leather sofas and overstuffed horsehair chairs. Stoneham sat behind an oak desk as big as the dugout, enveloped in cigar smoke.

"I've got a young fellow here I think we should sign for the stretch drive," Durocher said. "He can't field or run, but he's as pure a hitter as I've ever seen. He'll make a hell of a pinch hitter."

"I suppose you'll want a bonus?" growled Stoneham.

"I do have something in mind," I said. Even Durocher was not nearly so jovial as he had been. Both men stared coldly at me. Durocher leaned over and whispered something to Stoneham.

"How about six thousand dollars," Stoneham said.

"What I'd really like . . ." I began.

"All right, ten thousand, but not a penny more."

"Actually, I'd like to meet Bernard Malamud. I thought you could maybe invite him down to the park. Maybe get him to sign a book for me?" They both looked tremendously relieved.

"Bernie and me and this kid Salinger are having supper this evening," said Durocher. "Why don't you join us?"

"You mean J. D. Salinger?" I said.

"Jerry's a big Giants fan," he said. "The team literary society read *Catcher in the Rye* last month. We

had a panel discussion on it for eight hours on the train
to St. Louis.''

Before I signed the contract, I phoned my father.

''No reason you can't postpone your studies until
the end of the season,'' he said. ''It'll be good experience
for you. You'll gather a lot of material you can write
about later. Besides, baseball players are the real readers
of America.''

I got my first hit off Warren Spahn, a solid single up
the middle. Durocher immediately replaced me with a
pinch runner. I touched Ralph Branca for a double; the
ball went over Duke Snider's head, hit the wall, and
bounced halfway back to the infield. Anyone else would
have had an inside-the-park homer. I wheezed into sec-
ond and was replaced. I got into thirty eight of the final
forty two games. I hit eleven for thirty three, and was
walked four times. And hit once. That was the second
time I faced Warren Spahn. He threw a swishing curve
that would have gone behind me if I'd been alert enough
to move. I slouched off toward first holding my ribs.

''You shouldn't throw at batters like that,'' I
shouted, ''someone could get seriously hurt. I'm dia-
betic, you know.'' I'd heard that Spahn was into medical
texts and interested in both human and veterinary medi-
cine.

''Sorry,'' he shouted back. ''If I'd known, I
wouldn't have thrown at you. I've got some good lina-
ment in the clubhouse. Come see me after the game. By
the way, I hear you're trying to say that *The Great
Gatsby* is an allegory.''

''The way I see, it is,'' I said. ''You see, the eyes of
the optometrist on the billboard are really the eyes of
God looking down on a fallen world—''

"All right, all right," said the umpire, Beans Reardon, "let's get on with the game. By the way, kid, I don't think it's an allegory either. A statement on the human condition, perhaps. But not an allegory."

The players wanted to give me some nickname other than "Kid." Someone suggested "Ducky" in honor of my running style. "Fats" said somebody else. I made a note to remove his bookmark between innings. Several other suggestions were downright obscene. Baseball players, in spite of their obsession with literature and the arts, often have a bawdy sense of humor.

"How about 'Moonlight'?" I suggested. ´I'd read about an old-time player who stopped for a cup of coffee with the Giants half a century before, who had that nickname.

"What the hell for?" said Monty Irwin, who in spite of the nickname "Monty" preferred to be called Monford or even by his second name Merrill. "You got to have a reason for a nickname. You got to earn it. Still, anything's better than W. P."

"It was only a suggestion," I said. I made a mental note not to tell Monford what I knew about *his* favorite author, Erskine Caldwell.

As it turned out, I didn't earn a nickname until the day we won the pennant.

As every baseball fan knows, the Giants went into the bottom of the ninth in the deciding game of the pennant playoff trailing the Dodgers 4–1.

"Don't worry," I said to Durocher, "everything's going to work out." If he heard me, he didn't let on.

But was everything going to work out? And what part was I going to play in it? Even though I'd contributed to the Giants amazing stretch drive, I didn't belong.

"Why am I here?" I kept asking myself. I had some vague premonition that I was about to change history. I mean I wasn't a ballplayer. I was a writer. Here I was about to go into Grade 12, and I was already planning to do my master's thesis on F. Scott Fitzgerald.

I didn't have time to worry further as Alvin Dark singled. Don Mueller, in his excitement, had carried his copy of *The Mill on the Floss* out to the on-deck circle. He set the resin bag on top of it, stalked to the plate, and singled, moving Dark to second.

I was flabbergasted when Durocher called Monford Irwin back and said to me, "Get in there, kid."

It was at that moment that I knew why I was there. I would indeed change history. One stroke of the bat, and the score would be tied. I eyed the left-field stands as I nervously swung two bats to warm up. I was nervous but not scared. I never doubted my prowess for one moment. Years later Johnny Bench summed it up for both athletes and writers when he talked about a successful person having to have an "inner conceit." It never occurred to me until days later that I might have hit into a double or triple play, thus ending it all and really changing history.

When I did take my place in the batter's box, I pounded the plate and glared out at Don Newcombe. I wished that I shaved so I could have given him a stubble-faced stare of contempt. He curved me, and I let it go by for a ball. I fouled the next pitch high into the first-base stands. A fastball was low. I fouled the next one outside third. I knew he didn't want to go to a full count; I crowded the plate a little looking for the fastball. He curved me. Nervy. But the curveball hung, sat out over

the plate like a cantaloupe. I waited an extra millisecond
before lambasting it. In that instant the ball broke in on
my hands; it hit the bat right next to my right hand. It
has been over thirty years, but I still wake deep in the
night, my hands vibrating, throbbing from Newcombe's
pitch. The bat shattered into kindling. The ball flew in a
polite loop as if it had been tossed by a five-year-old; it
landed soft as a creampuff in PeeWee Reese's glove. One
out.

I slumped back to the bench.

"Tough luck, kid," said Durocher, patting my shoul-
der. "There'll be other chances to be a hero."

"Thanks, Leo," I said.

Whitey Lockman doubled. Dark scored. Mueller
hurt himself sliding into third. Rafael Nobel* went in to
run for Mueller. Charlie Dressen replaced Newcombe
with Ralph Branca. Bobby Thompson swung bats in the
on-deck circle.

As soon as umpire Jorda called time-in, Durocher
leaped to his feet, and before Bobby Thompson could
take one step toward the plate, Durocher called him
back.

"Don't do that!" I yelled, suddenly knowing why I
was *really* there. But Durocher ignored me. He was
beckoning with a big-knuckled finger to another reserve
player, a big outfielder who was tearing up the American
Association when they brought him up late in the year.
He was five for eight as a pinch hitter.

Durocher was already up the dugout steps heading
toward the umpire to announce the change. The out-

---

*This is not historically accurate, but it may be "correct." It is the way the
story has always been printed.

fielder from the American Association was making his way down the dugout, hopping along over feet and ankles. He'd be at the top of the step by the time Durocher reached the umpire.

As he skipped by me, the last person between Bobby Thompson and immortality, I stuck out my foot. The outfielder from the American Association went down as if he'd been poleaxed. He hit his face on the top step of the dugout, crying out loud enough to attract Durocher's attention.

The trainer hustled the injured player to the clubhouse. Durocher waved Bobby Thompson to the batter's box. And the rest is history. After the victory celebration I announced my retirement, blaming it on a damaged wrist. I went back to Iowa and listened to the World Series on the radio.

All I have to show that I ever played in the major leagues is my one-line entry in *The Baseball Encyclopedia:*

W. P. Kinsella   Kinsella, William Patrick "Trip-
                  per"
                  BR TR 5′ 9″ 185 lbs.
                  b. Apr. 14, 1934, Onamata, IA

	G	AB	H	2B	3B	HR	HR%	R	RBI	BB	SO	SB	BA
1951													
NY N	38	33	11	2	0	2	6.0	0	8	4	4	0	.333

I got my outright release in the mail the next week after the World Series ended. Durocher scrawled across the bottom: "Good luck, kid. By the way, *The Great Gatsby* is *not* an allegory."

DANIEL McAFEE

BATTING 1.000

They say I was the greatest pitcher of all time. They say that on that last day there wasn't a man in the universe that could hit me and I've let them say that all these years knowing it's a lie.

I'm old now. All the glory's gone out of it. It's all been unbelieved, if that's a word. It's all become just so much trivia and late-night, barroom reveries between old fans. Yeah, it's all a memory now; but I was there. I know what happened.

My name's Don Moore. I played for the Padres when they were in San Diego. I broke into the majors in 1987 and in the next ten years I won 310 games. By 1997 my arm was just a shadow of its former self and they moved me to relief.

Nobody can take those ten years away from me. Nobody can take away the summer of '90 when I started the season with ten straight shutouts: ninety-four innings without allowing a run to score. Nobody can take away the eight no-hitters I had in those ten years, the perfect game in '91, the night game in '89 when I struck out twenty-three of twenty-nine batters. Nobody can take away that season in 1992 when my ERA was 0.73 and I struck out 403 batters. Nobody can take away the two World Series rings of '91 and '92. *Nobody.*

By the end of that 1992 season my shoulder was in constant pain. Too many fastballs, too much hyperextension, too many years. Joints just aren't made to do what I did to mine.

The next four seasons were one long nightmare for me. I, who had lived by the fastball, had to develop a knuckler to get by, a sidearm curve to scare the daylights out of left-hand batters, a change-up to fool the hitters I used to blow away like August dust off the plate. I felt like a sprinter being forced to run the marathon. Each game was a war. I threw 200 pitches a game instead of the old 110, but I won. My fastball didn't jump anymore at 95 miles an hour like it had at 104, but I won. I struggled and sweated over each pitch, but . . . I . . . won.

The Padres of 1997 were the greatest team of all time. I don't think anybody will argue with that. Steve Cox, our leadoff man and shortstop, hit .385 on the season and stole 110 bases. John Eavy, second batter and second baseman, hit .368 and had ninety-four stolen bases. Then came the modern-day Murderers' Row: Harold Durr, our third baseman, fifty-four home runs; Tom Kurtz, our right fielder, sixty-five homers and a new record; Allen Scott, the only catcher in the dugout who could fathom my knuckler, fifty-seven home runs; Larry Lahr, our left fielder, fifty-one home runs; Rudi Rossy, ten-time gold glove first baseman; and Wayne Evens, our center fielder, longest arm in the majors.

Including Rossi, we had six gold gloves on the field

Richard Tomasic

and set the standard for the fewest errors in a season at
fifty-seven. The infield recorded 307 double plays. John
Satterthwaite took up where I left off and won thirty
games. Lee Byrd won twenty-seven. Bill Scudder and
Frank Wolder each won fifteen. Howard Curtis and I
saved seventy games between us. We won 131 of 162
games. We earned our way to the Championship, the
Series, the Ring Games. We earned it.

The Yankees didn't.

○ ○ ○

Ted Higman walked onto the field during spring
practice at Yankee Stadium. I heard about him second-
hand through Murray the scout even before the papers
got wind of him. Murray was a weasel. Most major league
scouts are old players who can't let go of the game, but
Murray was a real weasel, never played the game in his
life. He was a great scout simply because he didn't look
like one. He could get into places to see and hear things
no other scout could and Murray said Higman was a
hitter. Not like Ty Cobb, or Ted Williams, or Jackie
Robinson or even Pete Rose, but a hitter just the same.

Murray said Higman was skinny, maybe five feet ten
or so, and had big eyes. Very big eyes. Very big, very
yellow, very faceted, compound eyes like your average,
everyday housefly.

Murray, with a wave of his hand, said the story was
that Higman wasn't from Earth but from out there,
somewhere. He said that Higman and his friends used to
listen to our radio broadcasts on that other planet and

the '27 Yankees got him so fired up that he decided to come and give it a try himself.

He said Higman didn't have good foot speed, he wasn't powerful, he couldn't field the ball worth a damn, and he threw like a girl. But he could hit. He could hit singles like he was swattin' drunken ants on a picnic table.

He said Higman didn't know a thing about the game, only what he'd heard on the radio. He said the Yankees could only get two things across to Higman: hit anything that comes across the plate and run to first. Murray called Higman one ugly son-of-an-alien-bitch. The fans called him Flyman.

I, like most of the country, thought it was a publicity stunt to get the New York fans back to the stadium after two lousy seasons. I figured he was wearing some kind of goggles. I thought the Yankees had signed him as a designated hitter so they could pull him out of the dugout as a joke when the games were dull. I, like most of the country, was wrong.

That season is history now. The Padres were unstoppable with a winning percentage of .808. Yeah, we had a great season. A fan-damn-tastic season . . . but we took a back seat to Ted Higman, Flyman from outer space.

The Flyman batted 1.000.

○ ○ ○

The fans were split in two. They loved him and they hated him. They sent him bouquets of flowers and bottles of wine. Women jumped the walls to kiss him during the

games. Kids wore Flyman sunglasses when they played
ball. People who had never followed baseball began sub-
scribing to sports magazines and turning to the sports
page first in the paper. Real fans sprouted lightweight
headphones from their ears and were never seen without
them.

Many of these real, die-hard fans thought he was
ruining the game, much like the die-hard fans who came
before them thought the first black players had ruined it.
These purists sent him hate mail and phoned in death
threats. They threw things at him during the games and
shouted insults at him and his race and his mother. They
carried huge flyswatters to the games and wore T-shirts
that read "ET go home." Admittedly, some were just
kidding around, adding fuel to the fire . . . but some were
serious, very serious and very dangerous.

The Yankees hid the Flyman. He came to stadiums
like gold to banks. The New York management employed
several Flyman actors as decoys. Always, his location
was shrouded in mystery. The press never spoke with
him. The fans never got close to him for fear that those
who loved him would rip him apart for souvenirs and
that those who hated him would rip him apart for re-
venge.

But whichever stand the fans took on the Flyman,
all season long they packed the stadiums to see him play.

And all season long the Yankees' opponents tried
every defense in the book to stop him. They tried right
shifts and left shifts and running shifts while the ball was
in the air. They tried spitballs and beanballs and grease-
balls. Nothing could stop him. If the Yankees won the

game, it was protested. Their opponents said he had entered the country illegally; they said it wasn't fair to play against an alien who saw things with those weird eyes; they said anything, anything at all to rationalize the impossible fact that Higman could hit any pitched ball and place it as gently as a teacup anywhere on the diamond.

All season long the commissioner was barraged by phone calls from team owners and managers and players asking for rulings on contested games involving Higman. All season long he fended off scientists and government agents and reporters by the thousands. All season long he followed the Flyman's play and thought about what he could do to stop the corruption of the game. He thought about the friends the Flyman had left behind on the other planet and what might happen to baseball if a ship arrived full of flymen. He thought of how weak the Earth must appear to these aliens, beating us at our own game, on our own turf. He thought and he thought and he thought and he hid from the world hoping someone, somewhere would end the Flyman's perfect season, would strike him out and show the universe that the Earth could win when the chips were down.

And all season long the Flyman was front-page news. To the press he was gold, to the commissioner he was a danger to the game, to the fans he was excitement and to the greedy . . . a moneymaker.

Someone made a million dollars on a T-shirt with just a big black asterisk on the front, anticipating a Roger Maris-like decision from the commissioner on the matter of records by an alien. Someone wrote "The Flyman

Song" and made another million. There were Flyman
bats and balls and gloves and spikes. Flyman after-shave
and pantyhose and jocks—someone even made Flyman
condoms, cashing in with the play on words. The Flyman
was hot.

The Yankees struggled through the season and won
their division.

The Yankees struggled through the playoffs and won
the AL pennant.

The Flyman continued to bat 1.000.

It was destiny that we would meet.

It was destiny that the Series would go seven games.

It was destiny that I would come to pitch in that
seventh game, in the ninth inning, with two outs, one run
ahead, bases loaded, 70,000 screaming fans, tens of
millions watching, maybe billions listening.

The Flyman was up.

It had to be.

I had met him once before, in the third game, and
had walked him to get to a measly .280 hitter. But I
couldn't walk in the tying run now. I looked to the stands
as I warmed up on the mound. I saw the commissioner
in his private booth give me the thumbs-up, then he
smashed his palms together and blew as if blowing away
a dead fly. He smiled at me and I turned away with a
shudder.

I felt good. The fans were murmuring. I liked it
when the fans murmured. No one was going for beer or
hot dogs or pretzels. Everyone was waiting, waiting to
see me pitch to the Flyman.

○ ○ ○

I was ready. Coach patted me on the ass and left the field. I looked to the plate to get the sign from Allen and saw Higman's face: calm—calm as the Dead Sea. The stadium lights reflected off his eyes into a thousand tiny suns. I shook off the screwball. I felt good. I accepted the fastball.

I reached for that old juice, that old fire from the past. I wound up and burned one over the outside corner of the plate, right at the knees. A hush fell over the crowd as the speed was displayed on the scoreboard. I liked it when a hush fell over the crowd. The scoreboard read ninety-nine miles an hour, not bad.

"Steeerike one!" the umpire roared and the scanner confirmed, and the crowd screamed and the adrenaline pounded in my ears.

Higman smiled. He was playing with me.

I took the sign and looked at him smiling at me. I wound up and let loose a monstrous screwball right at his smiling face. He went down an instant before his face would have been mashed. Allen reached up nonchalantly and pulled the ball down. I dusted him. It could have meant the Series but I dusted his smiling, flyman face.

"Balllll one!" the umpire boomed and the scanner confirmed, and the crowd screamed louder.

Higman got up from the dust and smiled.

I took the sign and looked at the runners; they were smiling too. I wound up and uncorked the knuckler of all time, it danced and jigged and laughed and floated on its merry way. It rose two feet, dropped three, jumped and jerked and twitched on its path. It looked like it even stopped and fishtailed back toward me for an instant before it made its way to Allen's glove.

"Steeeeerike two!" the umpire bellowed, blue in the face, and the scanner confirmed, and the crowd screamed louder.

Higman smiled.

"Dear God in heaven," I prayed, "give me strength!" I took the sign. I reached down into myself for the One True Curve we all seek and let it fly. Allen dove and stopped it.

"Balllll two!" yelled the umpire, hoarse in the throat and the scanner confirmed, and the crowd screamed louder.

Higman smiled.

"Dear God in heaven," I prayed, "don't let me start crying. Let me strike this son-of-an-alien out. Please." I took the sign. There were tears in my eyes . . . just the wind. The stadium rocked and sang with one voice. I let loose the split-fingered fastball. Allen covered it in the dirt.

"Balllllllll threeeeeeee!" croaked the umpire and the scanner confirmed, and the crowd screamed louder.

Higman smiled.

That smile, that damn smile. I shook off the knuckler, I wanted to burn this guy. I shook off the change-up, the curve, the forkball. I wanted the fastball. My whole life for this one moment, this one pitch.

Allen turned to the ump and called time. The crowd groaned and began murmuring. Allen came to the mound to talk. Coach came out to talk, too. John and Steve and Rudi came over to talk. Harold even came over from third, and he hated meetings.

Allen said I should go for the knuckler, it was really

moving. Coach nodded and patted my ass. John said the dusting I gave Higman was a nice touch. Coach nodded and patted my ass. Steve said maybe the old blooper would surprise him. Coach nodded and patted my ass. Rudi said he liked it when the crowd murmured like this. Coach nodded and patted my ass. Harold said he had to take a leak and could we please hurry up. Coach nodded and patted my ass. "The fastball," I said, and they all nodded and patted my ass and went back to their posts.

The crowd stopped murmuring. I felt the weight of the thousands of eyes upon my back. This was no longer just a game to them or to those watching and listening across the world. Suddenly, even to those who had loved him, Higman became an invader testing our strengths and weaknesses. This was no longer a trivial game of skill, it was war in its most simple form: the best man of each side fighting it out to decide the winner for his people.

I looked into Allen's mitt. The silence was pure and heavy. Every beat of my heart roared loudly in my ears—as if in the silence the stadium had become one huge, human heart beating in the open air. And Higman, Flyman, stood calmly, straightly at the plate—an assassin's bullet of a batter.

Higman smiled and I breathed fire. My arm reared back, the fans stood on their seats, the ball touched my heel, the stadium skipped a beat, my front leg pointed to the sky, a murmuring began and spread like cancer, I came down: my shoulder hyperextending, my elbow dislocating, my arm whipping, my left knee touching the ground. The fastball of all time. Going for the sound barrier. A BB of a baseball. My motion was lightning and a murmuring thunder followed in its wake. The ball screamed upon its path and the fans were pitched into a frenzied roar that was heard for miles about the stadium.

Higman swung.

The ball popped into Allen's glove.

The stadium was graveyard still. Seventy thousand people standing, staring, silent. Higman staggered, unbelieving, his bat fell, and I could hear it hit the ground like a requiem. The utter silence was eerie. The scoreboard read 117 miles an hour. The pigeons cooed in the rafters and even the people in the top row in center field heard the umpire yell, "Yerrr out!"

Higman's uniform began turning red across his chest. I didn't understand. I looked at him and my thoughts raced back to a time when I had shot a rabbit and it had looked at me, just as Higman was looking at me, and the rabbit had screamed before it died—a high piercing scream of innocence.

Higman fell.

The dugouts emptied onto the field.

He'd been shot.

I struck him out and someone had shot him.

Someone had swatted him.

I thought of the jests of the commissioner.

I went to the plate like a magnet was pulling me. My arm was a noodle, something wrong inside of it, numb, dead at my side.

I dragged my eyes away from Higman's body and looked to the stands. The fans appeared frozen, waxlike in their surprise and shock. Movement caught my eye and I saw the commissioner just as he moved away from the stadium lights into the shadows of his booth.

Whatever spell had held the fans silent was suddenly broken and they stormed over the walls onto the field. They were everywhere, pulling hats and jerseys and hair. I grabbed Higman's bat with my good arm from where it had fallen and hit people with it. I bashed my way through the crowd toward the dugout. My eyes caught Allen's just as he went down, hands ripping off his mask and knee gear and spikes. I hit a screaming woman with the bat and Tom and Rudi pulled me into the dugout to safety.

The diamond was filled with crazed souvenir seekers. From the air it looked like spoiled meat swimming with maggots. In the stands fans ripped their seats out, they bent metal railings, they beat one another senseless for the rights to stray programs. On the infield, fans tore fistfuls of grass from the earth and fistfuls of hair from one another. They scooped up handfuls of dirt and held the dust high above their heads: treasured trophies. The bases were ripped to shreds. In the outfield Wayne and Larry ran for the fences. Larry made it over and ran through the back door to the dugouts. Wayne was pulled down along with the fence; the police found him wandering about the field the next day, naked and crying, searching for his mitt.

The hard, rubber home plate was torn to pieces along with the umpire and Allen Scott. Pieces of them were found about the field. Some pieces were never found. Their coffins were closed at their funerals; Allen's coffin held what was left of his body and his spare catcher's mitt. Someone put a ball-strike counter in with the umpire.

Nothing was left of the Flyman.

O O O

The Yankees contested the game and the commissioner convened representatives of both clubs in his office. I was in the hospital having the insides of my arm put back into place, and the commissioner didn't ask me to come to the meeting, he didn't ask me for a deposition or even for my opinion, he didn't ask me for anything. I learned about the conference secondhand from the papers.

The Yankees, claiming proof by exhaustive example, showed hours of films of Higman batting. In only one case did he ever miss the ball. In Atlanta, an irate fan had thrown a beer bottle at him while a pitch was on the way to the plate. Higman had hit the beer bottle in an effort to protect himself, shattering it and covering himself, the catcher, and the umpire with glass. The Yankees' preposterous claim was that Higman had seen the bullet coming in that last instant and had been distracted from his swing enough to miss the ball. One of the Yankee lawyers even went so far as to claim that Higman may have actually swung at the bullet instead of the ball.

The commissioner reviewed the film of the incident and found no evidence that Higman was aware of the bullet coming. No turn of the head, no gasp of fear, nothing but a light smile. He ruled that Higman had struck out and possibly faked the shooting to save face. He ruled that although he didn't believe life existed elsewhere in the universe, a new rule should be added to the books stating, "Only proven humans may participate in professional baseball on Earth." He ruled that on the season Higman had batted 1.000 but that the record books shall not log the record until and unless Higman or his family come forth to take the "human" test. He ruled that I had won my third World Series ring. He ruled that I had struck out the greatest batter of all time, and I've lived with the glory of that for all these years.

○ ○ ○

With no autopsy, they never were able to confirm that the Flyman was an alien. Soon, as is always the case, some people began calling the whole affair a hoax, a publicity stunt. They started saying that he was never shot, that the whole Series was fixed, that possibly even the entire season was a fraud. So many fans were on the field that the cameras were unable to see him trundled away, so they say.

But I know different. I know something I never told the commissioner, something I never told anyone until now: you see, I still have his bat, his bat with a bullet hole right through the meat of it.

W. J. HARRISON

GROUND RULE DOUBLE

at second
the runner is poised,
a cat on a fence,
balanced,
muscles held against their will
to run.
a backcracking sound,
the quick whiteness
slashes across the greenspace,
then that one true bounce
carries to the wall and beyond,
the moment
   lingers
in palatable relief,
the catlike runner
slows to third and around
   (the batter suddenly irrelevant)
   somewhere near second)
and scores the win.

ED CONNOLLY

DUMP THE DH

I'm greatly dismayed these days to find my name in such questionable repute. It has been linked to various catastrophies ranging from Armageddon bombs to black holes to disappearing ships . . . and now, the DH rule. Believe me, despite my overactive mind, I'm a traditionalist, and view tampering with the original laws of baseball akin to attempting to alter my special theory of relativity or atoms in interstellar gas: all three can be accomplished; however, the results are painfully artificial.

My name became involved with the DH several years ago when Stumpy Peitz (Heinie's nephew and a manager in the old "3-I" League) attempted to get the rule implemented. He felt that the DH would enliven a dying game; and he claimed to have endorsements from Eleanor Roosevelt, Albert Einstein, and, more recently, Prince. Not being aware of the views of Mrs. Roosevelt or Prince on the matter, I can assure you that I never added my name in support of the proposal.

As the years passed, colleagues at Princeton and throughout the international scientific community assumed that I was a great fan of the DH. The stigma has

49

followed me wherever I am recognized: "Oh, yes, there goes Albert . . . did you know that he formulated $E = MC^2$ and that he favors the DH rule?"

It is time to set the record straight. Our universe is an orderly and coherent creation. The physical laws governing God's perfection cannot be a chaotic collection of equations bearing only remote relationships to one another. As I've said time and time again, God does not play dice with the universe!

The designated hitter violates the cosmic order. An artificial intrusion into baseball is similar to disturbing the motion of the planets. A few years ago I used to tool around Jersey with Billy Martin, drinking beers and trying to make sense out of my unified field theory. I always insisted that the interrelationships among electromagnetic, nuclear, and gravitational forces are similar to the trinity of pitcher, batter, and fielder—all in the context of a set lineup with each position getting a chance at bat. Billy wasn't so sure.

As a physicist, I'm going to start actively campaigning against the DH in the following ways:

I was approached by a representative of General Mills recently concerning the possibility of their using my picture on boxes of Wheaties. It all has to do with their "scientists who love sports" ad campaign. The series will also include pictures of Eratosthenes of Cyrene, Newton, Copernicus, Carl Sagan, and Mr. Wizard on Wheaties boxes. I'm going to insist that my opposition to the DH be included in the biographical notes on all boxes.

In the future, whenever I call in on a radio sports talk show, I'm going to preface my questions or comments with a short diatribe against the DH. Finally, I'm going to write to the commissioner and let my feelings be known.

This crazy rule is so absurd and has become so far out of hand that, at times, I feel like creating a tremendous magnetic field around the whole American League and blasting it into another dimension. No wonder they are so lousy in the All-Star games.

Remember me from now on as Albert "Dump the DH" Einstein.

THE SPITBALL INTERVIEW: W. P. KINSELLA

Canadian born and raised (Edmonton, Alberta) and a graduate (with a MFA) of the University of Iowa's famous Iowa Writers Workshop, W(illiam) P(atrick) Kinsella is best known as the author of the highly acclaimed *Shoeless Joe,* one of the very best baseball novels ever published. When *Shoeless Joe* was published in 1982 as a Houghton Mifflin Literary Fellowship Award Novel, it swept through the literary baseball world like an Iowan cyclone, flattening mediocrity and setting a new standard for baseball fiction. *Shoeless Joe* even introduced a new kind of baseball fiction, called "magical realism" by its author, and practically overnight the novel made W. P. Kinsella a famous and magical name.

As is usually the case, however, Kinsella's "instant" fame and success is a false impression. By the time *SJ* was published, Kinsella had already established a reputation and earned a dedicated Canadian following for his short fiction, and particularly for his Indian stories. As a matter of fact, Kinsella had four collections of stories in print before *SJ* appeared: *Dance Me Outside*

(1977), *Scars* (1978), *Shoeless Joe Jackson Comes to Iowa* (1980), and *Born Indian* (1981).

Altogether, Kinsella has published over 200 stories, including over 100 about Indians, in magazines all over Canada and the United States. Of Kinsella's seven books published since *SJ,* two have been about baseball: his first collection of baseball short stories called *The Thrill of the Grass* (1984) and his second baseball novel, *The Iowa Baseball Confederacy* (1986). Both books earned Casey Award Nominations.

Happily, Kinsella is not one to rest on his laurels. He has told *Modern Fiction Studies* that just as "a

W. P. Kinsella

Blair Gibeau

baseball player is only as good as his last fifty at-bats, an author is only as good as his last book.'' Without fear of contradiction, we can say that no one, anywhere, is publishing more or better baseball fiction than Bill Kinsella, who lives with his wife Ann Knight (also a writer) in White Rock, British Columbia, just north of the U.S.–Canadian border.

sb: Bill, given the interest you've shown in baseball diamonds and stadiums in your fiction, what's your opinion of the domes? And particularly the Kingdome since you watch a lot of games there.

bk: Well, I have mixed feelings about them. I think they are necessary in some areas because of the bad weather. The Kingdome you get used to, I guess you can get used to anything after a while. There's some kind of problem with hearing. The sound doesn't get to you as quickly as it should, but after you watch a dozen or so games you sort of forget about it. Apparently, they have improved the dome in Minneapolis. I haven't been there since '82, and I swore I'd never go back because it wasn't air-conditioned and it smelled like a locker room after the third inning and it was hot and sticky and horrible.

Baseball's meant to be played outdoors in nice weather, but two years ago we were in Kansas City watching the Jays and Kansas City in the playoffs and we were wrapped up in all our clothes and a couple of blankets from the motel and umbrellas, and I turned to Ann and said, "Gee, wouldn't it be nice if this game were being played in the Kingdome."

So, I have a little sympathy on both sides.

Most places except California and Texas probably need a domed stadium for the first six weeks of the year. What are coming are the retractable roofs. Within fifty years, I suspect, almost every place where the weather isn't lovely will have a place with a retractable roof, and they'll be able to have grass if they want it. And they'll just close the roof up when the weather is bad. We probably won't live to see that, though.

SB: How important was the Iowa Writers Workshop to your career?

BK: Well, again, I had mixed feelings, but it gave me two years to write. They don't demand anything of you there, but I was mature enough that I wrote two books while I was there. And I wrote the first chapter of *Shoeless Joe,* actually in the form of a short story, while I was there, so it was probably my being in Iowa that precipitated my whole baseball-writing career. And it was the first time I'd ever been near major league baseball so that I didn't have to go miles and miles to see it. I was within driving distance of St. Louis and Kansas City and Milwaukee and Chicago and Minneapolis. So we saw a lot of baseball.

SB: Well, that explains the dust-jacket business about you spending summers "touring U.S. baseball capitals in a beat-up Datsun." Do you ever consciously look for story ideas at ballgames?

BK: I suppose I've come up with a few, and I've written some at games. I always carry a sheet of paper, and I always take a book to a game because I read between innings. I've occasionally written a little bit, not too often, but I read and I'll get a little idea and I make notes in the back of whatever book I'm reading.

sb: From our vantage point it appears that good baseball poetry is easier to write than good baseball short fiction. Do you have any idea why this appears to be so?

bk: Poetry is easier to write certainly. I mean good poetry is hard to write, but anybody and their dog can sit down and write "a" poem.

As far as I know, I'm the only writer writing baseball short fiction as really a genre. Lots of writers have written one story or so, but I appear to be the only person really working in that genre. I've got so many ideas I could never write them all down in three lifetimes.

sb: Well, getting to *Shoeless Joe,* where did you get the idea to put J. D. Salinger right in the middle of the story?

bk: The genesis of the novel is interesting because I wrote the first chapter almost exactly as it appears as a short story. I never intended it to be a novel. The story was published in an anthology called *Aurora: New Canadian Writing,* and the anthology was reviewed in *Publisher's Weekly.* I've never seen the review, but apparently there was a two-line mention of my story.

Now, a young editor in Boston with Houghton Mifflin, named Larry Kessenich, saw the two-line mention and wrote to me on the strength of it. He was right out of editors' school and didn't know that editors can't be bothered finding new writers, that they wait for them to come through the door. And he wrote to me and said, "We're all baseball fans here, and this idea of this man building a baseball diamond in his cornfield sounds so wonderful that if it's a novel we'd like to see it, and if it isn't it should be."

So I wrote back and said, "Well, I'm a well-established short-fiction writer, but I've never written anything successful longer than twenty-five pages. If I were going to write a novel, I'd have to have a good editor work with me." And at that point I started thinking novel.

And I knew that I wanted to write something about Salinger because everyone is curious as to what has become of him. So I thought I'd create what has become of him. And I knew that I wanted to write something about Eddie Scissons, and I knew that I wanted to write something about Moonlight Graham, and then I started thinking about turning it into a novel. And I thought, "All right, how can I tie these things all together?" And I went and reread everything of Salinger's and discovered that he had used two characters in his stories named Kinsella. And I said, "Ah, there's the tie-in. There's the tie-in."

My character wasn't named in the short story, so I said, "I'm going to name him Ray Kinsella, and there's the tie-in for him to go off and kidnap Salinger," and everything just rolled after that.

And Larry wrote back and said he would be willing to work with me, again not knowing that editors don't want to work with writers—they want the finished product to come over the transom. And so we only had one false start. *Shoeless Joe* was just like a baby. I wrote it in nine months. And it was virtually unedited.

SB: Is there a Kinsella in *Catcher?*

BK: Yes, there's a Richard Kinsella that Holden talks about in *Catcher* . . . the kid who rambled on and everyone in the class yelled "Digression" at him. Then there's a story called "A Young Girl in 1941 with No Waist at All," and the boy telling that story is named Ray Kinsella.

SB: And the interview in which Salinger confesses to having wanted to play in the Polo Grounds?

BK: That's fiction.

SB: Kind of thought so. What about Moonlight Graham? Did you conceive of such a character who had had only the shortest of cups of coffee and then search him out, or did you find Moonlight first and then decide to work him in somehow?

BK: It was a combination of that and sheer luck. I saw the name in the *Baseball Encyclopedia*—my father-in-law had given me a *BE* for Christmas that same year, I guess—and I stumbled on this entry and thought, "Moonlight Graham . . . I couldn't create a name like that." So, I said I want to write something about this guy . . . whether it'll be fiction or not, I don't know. I want to know if he sat in the bar for the rest of his life and got drunk and bragged about being a major league player, or how that cup of coffee affected his life.

You get ideas just by looking at where a guy was

born and where he died, and you find virtually no one who was born in the South who died in the North. If you come from a warm climate, you stay there. So, I thought, "Well, one of his sons or daughters must have been working up in the iron range and taken the old fellow up there to die." So I put two dollars in an envelope and wrote to the editor of the newspaper in Chisholm, Minnesota, and said, "Would you send me a copy of this man's obituary, and if you happen to know anything about him I'd be pleased to know it."

So she wrote back with the obituary and the editorial which she had written, part of which is quoted in the book.

And so we, that summer, Ann and I . . . first we drove up around where Salinger lives. We didn't make any attempt to contact him, but we drove up around Windsor, Vermont, and that, just to get the lay of the countryside. And then we went up to Chisholm, and it was just wonderful because Doc was the best-known citizen of the town and everybody over twenty-five had a Doc Graham story.

Virtually everything in the book is true about Doc except I invented how he got his nickname. No one had ever heard him called Moonlight. And he didn't talk about his baseball career; in fact, he was better known as having played amateur football than as a baseball player. A few people knew. Some thought he played for the Yankees, and some thought he played for the Giants, and all of them thought he played much longer than he had. But he never talked about it himself. And he was such a wonderful character!

We got just pages and pages of stuff, and I don't

remember what all I put in the book, but the thing I liked best was that he . . . when they tore down the old school where he had his offices, they found hat boxes with blue hats in them because his wife Alicia liked blue hats. The milliners used to get in blue hats because they knew Doc would go walking down the street and if he saw one he'd buy it. And so after he was retired he bought blue hats that he never got around to giving Alicia. He left an umbrella in every store in Chisholm, and people would say, "Now don't you touch that; it belongs to Doc. If it's raining, he'll come in and get it." And he gave away more free eyeglasses than should be legal in Minnesota and was just generally a wonderful, wonderful character.

And the most wonderful thing of all, of course, was I went into the newspaper office, talked to Veda Ponickvar for a few minutes, and said, "Do you know where I can get a picture of Doc?" I mean, I already knew there was a picture of him in his sixties at the library. But she turned and parted the ferns on her filing cabinet, and not only had a picture of Doc Graham but a picture of Doc in his 1905 uniform!

sb: Then Ann served in reality Salinger's role in the novel.

bk: Yes, she did Salinger's work, and I lurked in the background. She went out to the Country Kitchen where all the old-timers had coffee and got them all talking about Doc, and I just sort of lurked in the background. In fact, a year or two later, someone was talking to Veda Ponickvar at the paper, and she said, Oh, yeah, she remembered Kinsella and Salinger being there!

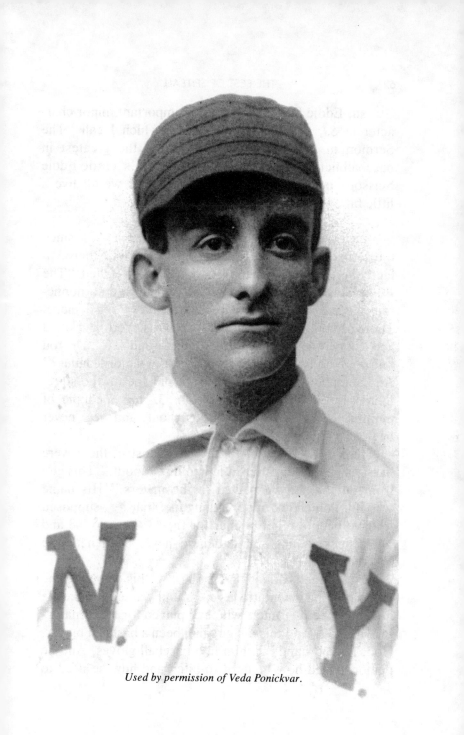

Used by permission of Veda Ponickvar.

sb: Eddie Scissons is another important minor character in *SJ,* and I think his scene, which I call "The Sermon in the Bleachers," is one of the greatest in baseball fiction. Would you say that there's a little Eddie Scissons in everybody, in the sense that we all live a little bit of a lie or an illusion?

bk: Well, I've had interesting experiences since then: there are a lot of Eddie Scissonses out there. In fact, there's a story in my new collection called "The Eddie Scissons Syndrome." I was going to do a nonfiction piece about it, but it turned into a fictional piece. There are a lot of old men who are liars. You go around and ask people—and you can do this—and say, "Do you know anybody who used to play in the major leagues?" And somebody'll say, "Oh, yeah, old Joe up the street there played for the Senators in '32 for a couple of months." And you check the guy out, and he's never been near the major leagues.

I've met several of these guys. Most of them were like this guy my brother-in-law told me about. "This guy from our hometown played in the majors." His name was Bill Pollichuck or something like that . . . supposed to have been a relief pitcher for the Yankees in '48 and '49. Checked him out, and he'd never been near the Yankees.

An eminent Canadian scholar . . . this woman came to my reading in Ontario last year and wanted to take me home to meet her uncle who had played for the Senators in '31 or '32. And this old guy had been a baseball player. God, he had hands on him like baseball gloves. And he demonstrated how he used to pitch and how he used to pick guys off first, and he was saying how the guys don't have good pickoff moves these days . . . and, gee, I went to the *Encyclopedia,* and he never had been in the majors. And he told me all about how he played for the Senators in '32.

And then I had the case I've semidocumented in the story. It was in Jefferson, Missouri, I believe. A doctor wrote to me and said, "I've got this patient in his nineties who claims that he played for the '17 White Sox and that he was the first black to play in the majors. When Charlie Comiskey found out he was black, he kicked him off the team. But he did get to play one full round of the league before they found this out. And he claims they destroyed his record."

And I said, "Well, it'd be just like Charlie Comiskey to do something like that, but you can't hide the back issues of the *Trib.* I can check it all out." So I sent a list of questions for him to ask this old guy, and the guy didn't come through. He named players that he played with everywhere from 1917 to 1940. He didn't check out at all. Yes, there are a lot of Eddie Scissonses around.

That whole thing came about because I was standing on the corner of Burlington and Gilbert in Iowa City one day waiting for the light, and this old man sorta poked his white cane in my navel and said, "Can you tell me the time?" I said, "Yeah, it's five to two." And he said, "Good. I got five minutes to catch my bus." He said, "Did you know I'm eighty-seven years old, and I used to play for the Chicago Cubs?" And I said, "No, I didn't know that." And my interest, of course, was monumental. I was thinking, "God, this guy's got to be the oldest living Chicago Cub. I'll phone Ernie Banks, who was the public relations man then, and surely he'll want this guy to throw out the first ball, and I'll get to go up with him, and there'll be an article for the *Trib* and something for the Cubs program and maybe a piece for *SI* and all this stuff.''

So, I got the guy's name and address and made arrangements to go interview him, and then I was right by the public library, so I ran into the public library and got out the *BE*, and not a thing. This old dude was a storyteller, just like I am. And so I didn't keep the appointment.

SB: That's funny! It's amazing how many of those fellows don't know about the existence of the *BE*.

BK: That's right.

SB: Or don't know that we know of its existence.

BK: No, I'm sure that they don't know of it. . . . There are a lot of them around.

SB: All these Eddie Scissonses sound like the modern equivalent of the eighteenth-century travel liars who wrote about places they'd never been to because travel writing was so popular. Our friend Percy Adams, who used to teach at the University of Tennessee, wrote a book on them called *Travelers and Travel Liars: 1660–1800*.

But getting back to *SJ;* in the scene in which Ray Kinsella talks to old Doc Graham, Moonlight says to Ray, ''This is my favorite place in the whole world. I don't have to tell you what that means. You look like the kind of fellow who has a favorite place. Once the land touches you, the wind never blows so cold again. You feel for the land like it was your child. When that happens to you, you can't be bought.'' What's the significance of Doc Graham feeling for Chisholm the way Ray feels for Iowa?

BK: That was kind of a coincidence because Graham did feel that way. I mean, here you have a Southerner who went North and was not feeling well one time . . . he had been playing ball . . . I'm not sure where . . . but anyway he was in Rochester for some reason, and they said, ''Why don't you take the train to the end of the line,'' which happened to be Chisholm at that time. And so he took the train up there and sort of fell in love with the place. They were rebuilding the place after a fire, and so he stayed there the rest of his life and really loved it.

SB: Well, what about the importance of place for writers? Do writers have to have a strong feeling of place? If they do, does it make an important difference in their fiction?

BK: Oh, yeah. I think it can't help but help if you have a place that you have feelings for. I've never had any feelings for a place before I went to Iowa. I lived in Alberta, was raised in Alberta, and it's a horrible, cold, ugly place. And I've lived on the coast, and I do like it very much here in the Pacific Northwest, but I don't have a terrible affection for it. I could move away from here and not feel any regrets. I like Iowa very much, though.

I like the South. I think that must be one of the reasons why so much good writing comes from the South

. . . because there's such a terribly strong sense of place there. It's so lush; the land is so much more of a force. I mean, I wish I were a Southerner. I would love to spend a lot of time in the Carolinas and Georgia and Mississippi. And Louisiana. If I wrote under another name, I think I could pass for a Southern writer, if I set stories there. I do have one story set in the South, but if I tried to do that now for a longer piece, people would say, "Here's this carpetbagger trying to usurp our land."

SB: Okay. I want to ask about one of the stories in *The Thrill of the Grass*. There is some wonderful self-parody in "The Night Manny Mota Tied the Record," but I'm a little puzzled about the ending. Can you say why Mr. Revere turns down the narrator when he finally offers to sacrifice his own life in order to bring Thurman Munson back to life? Aside from the obvious impossibility of a first-person narrator dying.

BK: Well . . . whatever information Mr. Revere was getting from his computer or whatever he had in his briefcase said that he couldn't take the guy no matter how . . . no matter if he wanted to or not. I don't know that it goes any further than that.

SB: It's just one of those inexplicable mysteries of fiction?

BK: That's right. He just wasn't the right person, and that's all there was to it.

SB: Okay. I just wanted to make sure I wasn't missing something.

BK: There's a little . . . I don't know whether it's parody or what of Salinger in there, of course, because of the fat lady . . . in *Franny and Zooey* everybody loves the fat lady.

SB: Oh, sure. I did miss that. One of my favorites in the collection is "Bud and Tom" because it demonstrates how successful a baseball story can be when it doesn't involve any play-by-play. In fact, there's no baseball at all in the story except for a single ball that is only referred to as "rotted back to earth," and that ball doesn't even enter into the story until near the end. Yet the story couldn't work without the baseball. Do you agree?

BK: Yeah, that's probably right. That's a strange story. It's the story people like least in the collection, I think. I write very little autobiography, but that is a fairly autobiographical story except for the baseball. The funeral scene and all that is right out of real life, and these two uncles of mine hated each other with a terrible passion, and no one knows what they fought about. I phoned my mother, and she claims she doesn't know, but I suspect she does. So I had to invent the baseball which is more wonderful than anything else they could have fought about.

SB: We don't really have the opportunity to go into *The Iowa Baseball Confederacy* in much detail here, but I would like to ask if you think the critics and commentators have missed or underestimated the extent of its parody.

BK: Yes, it's been reviewed with terrible seriousness in a lot of quarters. We must have had 120 reviews of that thing, and I don't think there have been more than two or three who have said, "This is a very funny book." I consider myself a humorist, first and foremost, and there are some very strange and, I think, very funny things going on in that book. Right from them taking Gideon as a mascot to all the stories Marylyle tells about Johnson County to the Black Angel to the Twelve-Hour Church to all these things. Yeah, this book has been reviewed with terrible seriousness. Some people like it, and some don't, but they're looking for profundity where a minimum of it exists.

SB: What are your favorite baseball books by other writers?

BK: I like Boswell very much, his *How Life Imitates the World Series* and *Why Time Begins on Opening Day*. Fictionwise, there's this book called *The Celebrant* which hasn't gotten any of the exposure it deserves. It was published with some outfit (Everest House) which sent it right into the remainder stores instead of the bookstores.

SB: What do the legions of fans of your baseball stories and novels have to look forward to next?

BK: I have a second collection of stories coming out in 1988 that is tentatively titled *The Further Adventures of Slugger MacBeth*. I've got another novel that's peripherally about baseball. It's a picaresque novel about an ex-ballplayer. It's called *If Wishes Were Horses,* and it's sitting with my agent at the moment.

I'm writing another baseball novel that will be a South American baseball novel . . . if I ever get it done. It's called *Butterfly Winter*. I've got about 100 pages of it written.

I've got so many short-story ideas, but the money is in the novels, so one of these days if I need money I'm gonna have to sit down and finish this *Butterfly Winter* novel. But I'm much happier writing short fiction. That's what I really like to do.

ROBERT L. HARRISON

THE HELLENIC LEAGUE

They uncovered the site
of that old ballpark,
where Homer once
recorded the scores.

The burn marks from
Mercury's slides still
scorched the earth,
and "Pop" Zeus'
footprints were
found in the
home team's dugout.

The section where the Sirens
sang their songs
(after the visitors got on first)
was found near the
gyro stands by the wall
that Hercules once called
"the marble monster."

What shots must have flown
from Apollo's bat.

What glory after
the Trojan nine was creamed.

The nectar poured
from Bacchus's concessiòn stands
after Hades threw
his famous heater
and Vulcan etched in stone
the final out.

The most marvelous find
was a Grecian urn
that turned out to be
a season's pass.

Shibe Park Philadelphia

Darryl Lankford

GENE FEHLER

THE DOME AND THE HALL OF FAMER

1

When Darden saw Springer make the signal for a pitching change, he turned his back to the infield and glanced up toward where the sky should have been.

The blue above his head was not sky, and no clouds drifted across it. No wind blew through the outfield to push fly balls above the home-run line that horizontally split the outfield wall; no breeze helped to keep fly balls in play. The thirty-mile-an-hour gusts so familiar back in Wrigley Field when he had first come up, and even before, when he was a kid in the bleachers, cheering Dave Kingman's soaring home runs, were now only distant memories.

"Three more outs," Darden mumbled to himself. "Let's get these last three outs and get the season over with. Then I'm done with it."

In twenty-one years of roaming center fields around the country, Darden had been as good as they came. As good as Speaker, DiMaggio, Mays. He could switch-hit with Mantle's power, and he had the Mick's speed. Best of all, he had stayed healthy.

Twenty-one years in the big time, Darden was a cinch Hall of Famer. And unless the Pirates rallied in the ninth, he had already seen the final at-bat of his career. His career totals would read, in part, like this: 4,423 hits; 728 home runs; 1,367 stolen bases. No one ever had those kinds of stats, not the combination of average and power and speed for so many years. Darden's exploits covered the most space in the record books of any player in history.

Three more outs and his career totals would be officially complete and ready to commit to memory.

"Come on Spokes!" Darden shouted as Carter Newsome finished the last of his warm-up throws. Carter had been "Spokes" for the past eight years. Darden had given him the nickname himself when Carter set a major league record of 128 relief appearances in one season. That had been seven years ago, the Cubs' last championship season. Carter had been the spokes in the wheel of the pitching staff. He had remained "Spokes" and the two men had been roomies ever since. They were, in fact, the only two players still remaining on the Cubs' roster from that championship season.

For that they had the club owner, Curry, to thank.

2

"Curry, you might have the fans fooled and you might have the writers fooled, but don't think for a minute you have the players fooled. These guys just won a World Championship for you, for God's sake, and look how you're rewarding them." Darden was starting to sink into the quicksand of carpet in Curry's office. Curry was a cheapskate, Darden thought, but not when it came to furnishing his office with the most luxurious furniture and carpeting made.

At the time of this meeting with Curry, Darden was in the middle year of a fifteen-year contract; he was secure for another seven years. Spokes had just signed a ten-year contract. Three other Cubs were in the middle of five-year contracts. The front office, however, refused to give any of the other Cubs a contract of more than one year.

"I want another championship," Darden said, "and if you don't sign those guys, we won't have a prayer."

"They're old," Curry snorted, lighting a four-dollar cigar. "This was their last hurrah." He paused after each sentence, punctuating it with a puff of heavy smoke. "There isn't a one of them who's got three solid years left. We're going for youth; we've got to build. You know that, Darden. Use your head, not your heart. We've got to build around you and Newsome."

"Bull! You're trying to save a dime, and the world knows it. We've got some young talent. Look at Banning. And Kendrick. They'll be stars in this league for ten years or more. You don't give a holy damn about a championship. You know that our fans will support us no matter what kind of a team you put out there. And if they suddenly stopped supporting us, you'd just unload us for a big profit."

"I wouldn't complain. You still have seven fat years left on your contract."

"Signed before you took over, or I'd be gone. You're stingy and you're a fool, and God help this club, and God help me and Spokes because we're stuck with long-term contracts, and anywhere you want to trade us, we'll be happy to go."

But no trade had been made. The Cub fans would put up with a lot; they would put up with almost anything short of a trade that would take their beloved Darden from them.

So Darden and Spokes stayed, two superstars on a team of seven straight second-division finishers.

3

And now, in Darden's final season, his final game, the Cubs were locked in fourth place again; this game was just to play out the string.

Spokes' slider was too high in the strike zone, and Darden knew before the swing what would happen, so he had already taken two strides toward left center before Banning, his old teammate, slammed the deep drive into the gap. Darden sprinted toward the wall, felt the warning track under his feet and leaped. His gloved hand speared the ball just before he rolled off the wall.

In twenty-one years of roaming center field, he had mastered the art of rolling off the wall. No matter what speed he was traveling when he hit the wall, he was always able to spin or twist and seem to slide with the wall instead of slamming into it. He touched the wall softly, like a father holding his baby for the first time, and he never got hurt by walls.

Darden hurried the throw back in, and the runner couldn't dawdle getting back to second. Then Darden trudged through silence back to his position. Not too many years ago, the crowds would have cheered such a play and he would have turned and tipped his cap and

grinned. Now there were no crowds. Now big league
baseball was played only to carefully screened media
people and to the television cameras that were being
operated by technicians with special security clearance.

Darden had lasted through the riots that had started
in earnest six years ago. Many of the stars of the game
had been seriously injured, four players had been killed,
and many more driven in terror from the game by rioting
fans.

At first, the rioting didn't seem worth worrying
about. Crowds had been growing more unmanageable for
years, and the players had been pushing for tighter
control. But the overzealous fans pouring onto the field
after almost every game had been tolerated by owners
running scared, even though fields had been torn up and
many games forfeited. Management had allowed the fans
to run at will; that is, until the Tolliver incident.

4

"They got to do something about those mobs."

"You said it. I'm just glad we weren't in the field
when this thing ended."

The Cubs were showering in the safety of the Indi-
ans' visitors' clubhouse, while above them thousands of
Indian fans celebrated victory. Since the Indians' switch
from Cleveland and the realignment of leagues, the ri-
valry between the two clubs was among the most intense
in baseball. But this was still only July and this game
didn't have any immediate pennant significance, so the
wild rush of fans onto the field was not totally expected.

"Someone's going to get hurt. Every game is getting

worse. One of these days some player isn't going to get back to the dugout in time.''

Similar conversations had been going on all year in numerous ballparks, but this is the conversation that was most remembered, because twenty minutes later the battered body of Indian outfielder Andy Tolliver was found on the artificial grass in short left field. He had been kicked so severely that his broken bones numbered in the dozens.

"Jesus! Tolliver is one of the most popular players here!''

The Cub players, collectively, shuddered.

Tolliver survived, but he never played baseball again.

Immediately, the security forces around the league were increased six-fold in an attempt to keep fans off the field after the games.

But then the throwing began in earnest. The stands rained golf balls, marbles, eggs, stones. Players took to wearing batting helmets on defense, but helmets weren't always enough.

Darden himself escaped serious injury twice, once when a hunting knife was hurled from the stands and missed him by inches. A second near miss came when he backed to the wall to make a routine catch, and a middle-aged woman pulled a small-caliber handgun from her handbag and shot at him. Luckily, she got only one shot off before someone knocked the gun from her hand. The bullet went through the fleshy part of Darden's side, just missing ribs and vital organs, so Darden didn't miss much action.

Security forces were increased again, fans were

warned, games forfeited, players were injured, but no one in a position of power seemed willing to take strong action. Not until Paul Pender.

Pender was right fielder for the Tigers, a four-time All-Star off to his best start ever. Though only one-fourth into the season, Pender had already hit a remarkable twenty-two home runs and was hitting .430.

Those statistics were part of the reason the entire baseball world was so stunned and outraged when a teenage boy stood by the right-field wall when Pender took his position in the sixth inning of a game against the Angels and, in front of fifty thousand fans, blew Pender apart with a hand grenade.

5

Shouts from infielders and coaches seemed to roll from the domed roof of the stadium and down toward Darden, waiting. He felt as if he were a museum piece, or perhaps part of the living dead, wandering around on the floor of a mausoleum. He watched Spokes slip a third strike past the pinch hitter, Murray, and he was glad there was only one more out. He felt sorry for the eight teams that still had to play in postseason games.

Darden had loved those championship series. He had been in nine of them and had emerged four times as a World Champion. But that had been years ago, when baseball had been played in front of screaming fans— baseball fans, not animals, not killers—when baseball was a pastime and when spectators loved the game for the game itself and when there was grass and sky.

Now playing a game was like writing a letter that no

one would read. There was an incompleteness about it, a feeling of discontent, a feeling that what he was doing had no meaning anymore. Darden was forty years old and over half of those years had been spent playing baseball and hearing cheers. There were no cheers now, and even the remembered cheers were muffled in his mind. The faces of fans were hazy.

For a moment he saw the faces as they had been in the years after the Pender incident. All big-league parks had built transparent bulletproof partitions to separate the fans from the players. The partitions were sound-proof; the fans could be seen but not heard. It had scared Darden to look at the fans. Their mouths were open wide and they gestured frantically. It was as if they were crazed, caged, or perhaps caught in Dante's Inferno. One of the strongest images that remained was that of the fans giving the players the finger. Even young boys and girls only seven or eight years old had mastered the obscene gesture.

The partitions had worked moderately well for less than three years. Then the fans started throwing things toward them: fruit, eggs, garbage. All forms of messy, smelly refuse smeared and streaked the partitions. And when fans tired of throwing garbage, they fought each other, until eventually two separate games were being played at once—one on the field, one in the stands.

This past season was the first in which everyone had been banned from the ballparks—everyone, that is, but the technicians and the media. Ratings were higher than ever for TV broadcasts, the public was still watching baseball; and the revenues earned through pay-TV and radio would keep baseball more solvent than ever.

But for Darden, it wasn't the same. It could never be as good. He was glad he had played when he did. How terrible it would be to be a rookie just coming up who would never know the thrill of sliding on real grass to make a catch and of hearing the love of sixty thousand fans pour over your head and down through every fiber of your being.

One out away from retirement, Darden heard the bat strike the ball for the final time in his long career. The ball was hit high toward medium-deep center field. Darden came in a step, looked up into the blue sky and watched the ball drift down. It was not really blue sky, of course; it was dome-painted imitation sky, just like every other stadium in the big leagues. Every park identical in dimensions; every park totally laid out with artificial grass, every park with a sky-blue painted dome.

Some parks used to paint clouds on the roof of the dome to make the illusion of sky more realistic, but other teams complained, so the commissioner ruled that every dome must be painted an identical shade of blue. Now stadia were exact duplicates, clones.

The ball dropped from the clear imitation sky, and Darden caught it easily. He jogged toward the dugout over the imitation grass, and no fans were there to tell him they were glad for the twenty-one years he had given them.

Darden handed Spokes the ball.

"Well, it's over," Spokes said.

"Yes," Darden said.

Spokes and Darden stood together outside the dugout until the field was deserted.

"It won't be the same without you," Spokes said. "You're not old. You could play three or four more years easy."

Darden shook his head. "We've been all over that," he said.

"You're all that's left from the good days," Spokes said.

"You could quit too," Darden told him. "You don't have to go on."

"I need the money."

Darden nodded. The two men stood side by side in silence for a long time. Darden watched the domed sky, waiting. Finally the lights of the stadium died. The sky was dark.

"It's not baseball, Spokes. Not anymore."

Spokes' fingers caressed the seams of the baseball he was holding. "What the hell," he said.

They left the field together, and Darden sat down in front of his locker to undress. The season was over. Everyone except Spokes and him had already gone. There would be no emotional good-byes.

TIM PEELER

CURT FLOOD

try to tell 'em Curt,
how you crowned their wallets,
climbed courtroom steps
for them,
swallowed that black ball,
a scapegoat out to pasture.
they don't remember,
can't remember
the trash you ate,
your greedy headlines,
the slope of your career.

you are a ghost at barterer's wing,
your smokey gray eyes
are two extra zeroes
on every contract.

ROGER KAHN

THE REPORTER

(A great writer remembers the man and his ordeal: Roger Kahn reminisces about "Pursuit of No. 60: The Ordeal of Roger Maris," Sports Illustrated, October 2, 1961. Recorded in Cincinnati, August 17, 1986.)

When the article began both Maris and Mantle had a shot at Ruth's record. And I went out to cover both Mantle and Maris pursuing Ruth. Mantle dropped out (when he passed Gehrig at forty-eight he said to Roger, "I've got my man."), and the press began to swarm. Eventually, there would be sixty people covering Maris. And I would keep notes on the dumbest questions: somebody said, "Do you play around on the road?" Which was then not usable. Maris said, "That's my business." And the reporter said, trying to get him to talk, "I play around on the road." Maris said, "That's your business." Somebody else said, "Would you rather hit sixty home runs or bat .300?" And then he'd hit a breaking ball, and the reporter said, "Was that ball breaking in on you?" And Maris said, "Well, seeing as how he's a right-handed pitcher, I'd say, 'Yes.' " And then there were little moments . . . Maris said something about "the damn reporters," and Elston Howard in the next locker said, "If I had fifty-three home runs [or whatever it was] I wouldn't be complaining about the reporters."

The sense was that Maris didn't want to be changed by this, and of course he couldn't avoid it. So he couldn't go to a delicatessen in New York where he liked the sandwiches . . . and be left alone. The experience was frightening to him. He said, "They bust in on me even in church." So I focus on one man in the middle of this extraordinary streak with a growing press. And he's comfortable being what he was, but he can't be what he was anymore. So that's sort of the thrust of the piece . . . the change is frightening, here is this frightening change . . . he tries to be a typical ballplayer, but he's no longer a typical ballplayer.

There was one night in Detroit when he wouldn't come out and meet the press. I think he'd gone hitless in a double header, and he sat in the trainer's room with his brother. And a reporter says to Ralph Houk, "How can his brother be in there and I can't?" And Houk says, "You're telling me I can't let a man's goddamned brother talk to him?"

Maris never really blew up, and he wasn't as difficult as he's been depicted. Give him time . . . and there wasn't much publicity help in those days. So he had to pretty much do it on his own.

And the following spring I saw him and he said with great geniality and seriousness, "Of all the horseshit that was written about me last year, yours was the best." You take literary criticism where you find it.

EUGENE C. FLINN

NEVER MIND "WHO'S ON FIRST?"; WHO'S IN THE OUTFIELD?

"*B*all three. High and on the inside. The count is three and two and with two outs the runners will be going."

The television image flickered as a plane passed overhead. Grumps took a long sip of his Bud, icily encased in a tall pewter mug. This was the Cardinals' best opportunity of the night. They were down 2–0, but a base hit could tie the score. A single that took its time getting to the outfield could clear the bases and put St. Louis ahead. Pete Rose had knocked in three runs against the Mets on a single earlier in the year.

"C'mon, Herr. You can do it. Belt it out of the park."

Gooden eyed Willie McGee taking a careful lead off first. He had been picked off in the seventh in a situation like this and he was being cautious. Gooden tossed over to Hernandez and McGee got back easily.

"C'mon, Tommy," Grumps entreated from the sofa of the Finneran living room. "Just get a piece of it."

Tim McCarver was announcing, a hint of Memphis, Tennessee, in his voice.

"The ballgame could ride on this pitch, folks. Gooden takes a look at Tito Landrum on third. He steps off the mound. Here comes Gary Carter out to check the signals. What would you say, Ralph? Do you think he'll come in with a fastball?"

"It's power against power, Tim. And my money is on Gooden. Of course, Tommy Herr is probably expecting a fastball, so Dr. K might try to fool him with his curve."

"That's what makes baseball a game of guesses and inches, Ralph. Well, the umpire has had enough of this. Gooden is on the mound. Herr is preparing himself for the pitch."

Grumps knew Patti was busy writing and he had promised himself that he wouldn't bother her, but the tension was driving him crazy. As Gooden gave one last look at Carter, Grumps blasted out: "Patti, come here a second!"

Gooden let fly. It was a fastball. Herr, anticipating it, began his swing. Suddenly he held back.

"Did he swing?" McCarver screamed. "The first-base umpire says he came around. The game is over, folks. The Mets beat the Cardinals, 2–0. It's Gooden's fourth shutout. After his unbelievable stats in 1985, it looks like he's going to have another great season."

"And that's the tenth time the St. Louis Cardinals have been blanked this year," Ralph Kiner pointed out. "It's hard to believe that last year they led the league in batting and came within two outs of being the World's Champions. And here in '86 they are struggling.''

Grumps left his sofa abruptly, spilling some of his Bud in the process, and angrily shut off the television.

Patti, his wife, her cool blue eyes and soft flowing brown hair easing the gloom of the room, entered. Her thoughts were still with Alexandria chained hand and foot in the lonely mill by the Meuse River by the henchmen of the baron because she wouldn't tell the secret of the molecules—the point in the novel she was writing when Grumps called.

"And how are the Cardinals doing, dear? Are they defeating those awful Metropolitans from New York?"

O   O   O

"Another beer, Grumps?"

"Naw, I think I'll hit the hay."

Patti smiled sympathetically. "If you don't want a beer, would you like a cup of tea?"

"The last thing . . . the last thing in the world I want right now is a cup of tea."

Grumps saw the little hurt in Patti's eyes.

"I'm sorry, honey. It's just that the Cardinals have never lost so many times. I've been following them for years and I never saw a Cardinals team as bad as this. They haven't been this bad since 1918, the last time they finished last. And yet this is almost the same team that won the pennant just a year ago. And their pitching is probably even better now."

Patti, as slim and lithe as a rookie shortstop, put on

the Cardinals hat Grumps had bought when they watched
John Tudor shut out the Mets 1–0 in Shea Stadium last
year. She picked up the broom and she swept the hairs
that Dizzy and Daffy, the Finnerans' two golden retriev-
ers, shed daily over the living-room floor.

"Now batting for St. Louis," she announced,
"Tommy Herr. Here comes the pitch. He swings. It's
going, going, going . . . right over the fence for a
touchdown!"

The broom swung wildly through the air, hitting the
imaginary baseball with a resounding *crack!* from Patti's
lips and another one equally resounding as Aunt Milly's
Christmas gift, a porcelain vase in the shape of a swan,
crashed into a hundred pieces.

"I never liked that vase anyway. Did you,
Grumps?"

Grumps smiled despite himself. He had been think-
ing of attacking Aunt Milly's atrocity himself.

"That's the way, Grumps. Do you want to talk about
the Cardinals? Do you think it would help?"

"Okay Patti. But one condition. As long—"

"I know, Grumps. As long as I don't say it's only a
ballgame."

"Right."

Although the chains were tightening around Alex-
andria's wrists, and the bad baron was on his way, Patti
had to agree with her husband.

"Of course. Look, Grumps, life is not much longer
than an extra-inning game. I know that. Every time at
bat is important. Everything you do—even when you're
just standing in right field wondering if someone is ever
going to hit a ball your way—is important. After a while

you may forget the score of a baseball game or even who won, but those few moments right after it's over . . . Well, gosh, they stick to you like a tight-fitting girdle, right?''

Grumps looked at Patti in amazement. Most of the time he thought she didn't know what she was talking about when she was talking baseball, but there were times when he wasn't exactly sure. Right now, for instance, she seemed to be making sense.

"I think I know what's wrong with the Cardinals," she said. "I haven't had the chance to talk to you about this, but I wrote a letter to Whitey Herzog."

"Y-you what?"

"I gave him my theory on why his team was losing. I told him the Cardinals weren't being beaten by the Mets and Expos but by the moons of Jupiter."

"You're putting me on; there's no such team, not even in the minors."

"I didn't go into that too deeply, Grumps, because I didn't want to discourage him with a lot of scientific data, but I did point out that the planets had not been as good to him this year as in 1985."

"What do the planets have to do with it?"

"Grumps, it is a fact that cosmic rays are continually falling to the earth from the universe. We may not see them, but they're there, just like television waves. Some of the molecules in these rays are good for certain people; others are bad."

"So you wrote him that the Cardinals have been standing under the wrong molecules this year?"

"Maybe not in exactly those words, but that was the gist of it."

Grumps whistled. "And you actually wrote that to Whitey Herzog . . . all that stuff about the planets making him lose?"

"I also told him how upset you have been, you who have followed the Cardinals from Pepper Martin and Rogers Hornsby to Leo Durocher, Stan Musial, Country Slaughter, Bob Gibson, Lou Brock, and all those other Gas House players."

Grumps hated to see his heroes chronologically disoriented.

"Patti, Musial and Brock and Gibson were not with the old Gas House Gang. Frankie Frisch, maybe and Diz—"

"Whatever. But I pointed out how much you like his team. Told him I liked baseball myself because one of its most exciting plays was named after a Greek poet."

Grumps smiled. English had not been his favorite subject in college, but even he was familiar with Homer.

"Anyhow, I told him I was a writer and a researcher and that if he would give me a position in charge of the bats or something for a few days so I could sit next to him on the bench and advise him, I would guarantee him a little winning streak. I explained that once the Cardinals got into the winning habit again they could do it on their own because when they gain confidence in themselves they can fly on to their penance."

"You mean pennant."

"Whatever."

Grumps chuckled. "I can just picture old Whitey reading your letter," he said.

Pattie reached into her pocketbook. "He *has* read it; here's his answer."

She handed her husband a postcard with a picture of Busch Stadium on the front. He turned it over. The message was simple:

I'm so desperate I'll try anything. Meet me at Shea for the series with the Mets. Whitey H.

Most of the Cardinals greeted Patti's arrival with indifference. Since their series of losing streaks began, Herzog had been beseiged by psychics, fortune-tellers, faith healers, and shrinks, so the advent of a bat-woman, as she asked to be called, did not strike them as unusual. Ozzie Smith discovered she was interested in calisthenics and traded exercise tips with her; Vince Coleman accepted her challenge to a 440-meter race, giving her a handicap, and Danny Cox showed her how to throw a curve. What did startle the team, however, was the first advice she gave to Whitey Herzog in the ninth inning of the first Mets game.

The Cardinals were hanging on to a 13–12 lead, but the first two Mets had walked. Sisk, the Mets pitcher, was due up next and the Cardinals were expecting a bunt. Pattie, who hadn't said a word to Herzog throughout the game, rushed over to him and whispered in his ear.

"Put in a new pitcher so I have time to give you my strategy."

"Do you have any preference or can I use whoever I want?" he asked sarcastically.

"Oh, it doesn't matter. The blond-haired fellow would be nice."

Herzog signaled for Ken Dayley, who had been warming up.

"Now what?"

"Before I give you my strategy, Mr. Herzog, I must explain my overall philosophy, as it applies to the Cardinals' slump, that is."

Whitey shuffled his hat impatiently. "You've got to spit it out quick, Mrs. Finneran. The umpire only allows a few warm-up pitches."

"I'll be as brief as I can. In a nutshell, your team has been losing because they have been playing in the wrong places."

"W-what?"

"Does Willie McGee always have to be in center field, for instance? Couldn't he stand next to Tommy Herr once in a while?"

"Now wait a minute. McGee—"

"Look, Mr. Herzog, you know that every human being is composed of cells, right?"

"Y-yeah, but what's that got to do with McGee coming in from center field?"

"Everything. These cells are composed of the same elements that are in the stars, planets, comets—"

"Why did I get into this? Isn't being in last place punishment enough?"

"Place! . . . See, that's it! You're in last place because your players are in the wrong positions, next to the wrong molecules, causing the Cardinals to lose and my husband to get upset. Last year they were where the right molecules were most of the time. That's why they were winning. Look, if that umpire had been in a different place in the sixth game of the World Series last year, he might have called that Kansas City man out at first and the Cardinals would have won the championship, right?''

"Well, yeah. He blew—"

"Well, that's the point. You've got to put your men where the good molecules are. Bring Willie McGee in from center field and put him near Tommy Herr. Put Vince Coleman near third base where Terry Pendleton plays and put Tito Landrum near first where Jack Clark is. Then the first baseman and third baseman can play right near the plate to get the bunt. You'll get a double play."

"Are you saying to bring the entire outfield into the infield?"

"Is it against the rules? There are a lot of silly rules in baseball."

Whitey scratched his head. "As long as all the players except the catcher are inside the baselines they can play any place they want, but without an outfield they'll have Sisk swinging away."

"But my husband told me he's a pitcher and most pitchers can't hit very well. And the Mets have run out of pinch hitters."

The umpire gave the sign to play ball.

"You promised," Patti reminded Herzog, reading the doubt in his eyes.

"What've I got to lose," he said to himself, and beckoned the unbelieving McGee, Landrum, and Coleman into the infield.

Sisk, all set to move the base runners along with a bunt that would put the winning run on second, stepped out of the batter's box as he saw the infield surrounded by Cardinals. He had not played with so many fielders that close to him since the Pee Wee League. He looked over at third and got the sign to hit away.

When the Cardinal outfielders started to come in, few of the Mets faithful paid notice. They thought because of the length of the game and the flakiness of the Red Birds of late that Herzog had called time to remind his fly-chasers that they only had a one-run lead and where to throw the ball if it came their way. But when the fans realized that the outfield was actually lined up to play in the infield, the stadium exploded with hisses and catcalls.

"Who's on first?" a wit screamed out.

"Never mind that," another answered. "Who's in the outfield?"

Dayley, the Cardinal pitcher, threw him a fastball and Sisk missed it by a foot. Somehow the proximity of so many of the enemy so close unnerved him. He checked the sign and saw he was still asked to swing away. A little soft fly over the heads of Coleman, Smith, McGee, Herr, and Landrum, who were forming a picket line in the infield, would be enough to score one run, probably two. It would be impossible to bunt with Pendleton and Clark standing in front of him.

Sisk met the next pitch squarely and it rocketed over Coleman's head down the left-field line. The crowd roared, but the umpire on third base called it foul.

Whitey wiped beads of perspiration from his forehead. "Look, Mrs. Finneran, it was a clever idea, but I think I should send my outfielders back to their positions and force Sisk to bunt. If he fouls this one off, he's out."

"Remember what I said in my letter, Mr. Herzog,"

Patti said, smiling confidently. "You can control the moons of Jupiter if you have the courage."

Whether Herzog would have changed his mind, we will never know because he hesitated too long. Sisk swung at the next pitch, hitting a line drive to Ozzie Smith, who under the new alignment was playing right on second base. Ozzie stepped on the bag and fired a bullet to Landrum covering first.

Statisticians have been arguing ever since over whether this was the fastest triple play in baseball history.

○ ○ ○

The Cardinals swept the four-game series, with Patti suggesting movements of the players at key moments in all but the last game. By that time she had Herzog so convinced of the importance of lining up with the good molecules that he didn't question her, although in the final game she came up with the most bizarre suggestion of all, though not at a crucial time.

With two out, no one on, and Keith Hernandez up in the first inning, she told Whitey to bring the outfielders in again and to have them sit down near second base with the four infielders.

"Tudor will strike out Hernandez, so as long as the catcher doesn't drop the last strike, you don't need any other players," Patti explained.

"But why take the chance when a fly ball could be a home run?" Whitey started to say, but then bit his tongue. The dame had gotten him this far. Might as well give her a shot.

"You see, Mr. Herzog, the molecules are not working out well for Hernandez right now, especially since he is going to be trying so hard. And striking him out without any fielders behind him is going to give Tudor confidence for the rest of the game. And the rest of the season too, I hope.''

Hernandez whiffed on three curves and Tudor pitched a three-hit shutout, striking out the Mets' first baseman two more times. The Cards, as relaxed as spaghetti, won 12–0.

○ ○ ○

After the game Patti turned in her uniform to Whitey.

"I don't think you need me anymore, Mr. Herzog. Once a team starts winning, the players tend to find the good molecules by instinct. I think it might be a little psychological, too. They'll do better now and much better in 1987.''

Whitey nodded his silver head gravely.

"Well, it was a pleasure,'' he said. Then looking down at Patti's old uniform, he handed her the cap. "Take this for a souvenir. And here's a baseball for your husband.''

"Thanks, Mr. Herzog. Oh, just one more thing. How many pitchers do you have on your squad?''

"Nine, right now.''

"Good,'' she responded. "Just enough for a team. When you play the Dodgers next week let the pitchers play all the positions. They spend too much time in the dugout and on the pitcher's mound and need to get to the other places in the field to meet the other molecules.''

Whitey said he would give it a try.

C. BROOKE ROTHWELL

THE NEVER-BEFORE-COLLECTED WORKS OF BABE RUTH

*In baseball, the Babe Ruth signature
says it's the genuine article.*

Babe Ruth

NOTE: I have left the manuscript unaltered but have taken the liberty of including relevant newspaper clippings and interspersing them throughout the journal.

"It's late. This rum has the fireplace roaring and I figure I've got to start someplace so here goes. As long as I can remember I've been fascinated by the internal organs of my thumb. 'Course the thumb is the key word of the hand and the hand is the mirror of the soul which reflects what we pick up. Now what we pick up most often is the nature of our soul and duality being an intrinsic part of life, I'd like to distinguish between bats that fly and the

97

kind that I picked up most often that when swung sent
the spheroid up into the rarefied air of the unimaginable.
From the club of the caveman to the twentieth century,
this being 1927, I find myself to be the most singular
example of an uncivilized human being since the ape's
banana became a symbol of the male sexual organ (I've
heard that Eve's collection of bananas was deleated from
Genesis). Nobody, aside from afew hand chosen women
knows this side of myself, the internal side I mean. To
those of you who hold this document in your hands
consider it to be like the Dead Sea Acrolls, chapters of
which will never be included for the simple reason that
this is the 'inside dope,' as opposed to what you read in
the papers—the box score aside.

"The reason I supposedly didn't know anybodys
name is because they all knew mine."

CLIP: "The 'Baby Ruth' candy bar was mistaken
by some to have been brought out in homage to the Babe
but it was really manufactured for the benefit of Hoover's
newborn daughter, Ruth. When Babe was approached
on the subject he said, 'People believe what they want to
believe and that's the way it should be.' "

"My pal Rabbit Maranville was a perfect smoke ring
in outer space. We had alot in common Rabbit and me if
only because we spoke the same language, so to speak.
He's in the Hall because of his ears you know. Loved
me 'cause he could insult anybody knowing I'd hold him
back. If I could of written his tombstone I'd have chisled,
WHAT THIS COUNTRY NEEDS IS A GOOD 5¢ BIO OF THE
RABBIT."

"When the sun's in the oven, the grass is smoking and your glove smells like a roast . . . when your bat seems three miles wide, when a baseball game enters your blood stream the deepest philosophies of the most abstract thinkers becomes the baby's rattle of the riddle solved."

"My favorite flower is the blue rose. My favorite gal singer is Ruth Etting. My favorite entertainer is Houdini, Groucho Marx, his brothers, and Al Capone. My favorite food and drink is women and beer."

CLIP: "Man on the street circa 1920 when Ruth hit fifty-four home runs: 'Ya, I met the Babe once. It was outside the Bergoff in Chicago. I remember asking him what his advice to aspiring young ballplayers would be in one sentence. He said, "I'd tell 'em to use cornstarch in their jocks." ' "

CLIP: "As a rookie with Boston, Ruth was asked by a syndicated baseball writer off the record what his father did beside tend bar and Babe replied, 'He fucked every night.' "

"My only real painful regret is that I never had a child of my own. Too busy being one I guess. Boy, that would have been something! I got drunk over that alot."

"On liquor: I've woken up many times hugging the earth. To prevent people from drinking is like saying they can't dream. Fifty guys feel elected enough to dictate how 50 million will think. Politics like religion is mind control and I hate control because as the Marquis de Sade (who I read in France) pointed out, its against nature when nature is functioning properally, that is, freely within the constricts of possibilities. Man is perverse because he's free. His imagination is payment for this freedom.''

"Somewhere down the line I realized I could do whatever I wanted. It hit me when I understood other people couldn't or wouldn't. That's when I started to have fun and give other folks enjoyment to boot. Now, I didn't use this power against other people. Only pitchers.''

"I loved to cuss. Always thought that words like 'damn' or 'hell' had certain places in a conversation. See, those negative words hinted in a positive way, they expressed a certain kind of negation. 'Holy Shit' was an ironic phrase that implied a sort of agreement with something that can't be expressed any better any other way. I never took the lord or any other word that possessed unconsciously charged conotations for granted or in vain.''

"Cobb was a real gem of a prick. A truely great ball player in the incredible sense but when you understood why he acted the way he did on and off the field he became for those who knew or played with him something of a freak. His competitive nature reduced most players to maniquens. Pure intimidation. Used to call me 'nigger' 'cause of my nose. A real asshole. But it was a joy to make him laugh. He died hard. His way.

"When I think of death I think of the ballpark of God's imagination. I'll be hitting 'em out where ever I go.''

O O O

"Regarding my throat cancer: I think tobacco is a spirit infested with many demons that speak to portions of our brain that inspire us to become who we are and will be. We kill tobacco by burning it and it relinquishes its secrets which inspire our own death. But not before becoming inspired by the earth it draws its inspiration from. I really love it and had Clair arrange to have a cigar placed in my coat pocket upon burial. Its the Egyptian in me!

"The years with Clair were hard. Especially at first. But she brought me what I needed, especially towards the end; a sence of establishment of belonging, because I thought I was going to last forever. Put yourself in my shoes. . . . If you dare break the glass upstate in New York."

"The subject of Jesus was drummed into me for a long time. But actually, as much as I agreed at a tender age with this tender guy, I later agreed with myself on the fact that he had his life and I had mine. People who tell other people how to live are posessed with a certain truth it seems. At this stage I don't give a damn about Jesus (only Brother Matthias would really understand) because he doesn't give a damn about me to the point that I have to give a big damn about myself and that's what I think he was saying anyway. Fact is, the closest anybody is gonna get to whatever they think God is, is their deepest level of consciousness; their most honest relationship with themselves. I don't even like to think about Jesus. Its like UFO's . . . and then there's my total lack of respect for authority!"

"Somebody asked me when I was real young what I wanted to be when I grew up. I was so struck by the idea that I instantly put it out of my head. I think because I never wanted to do anything 'cept play ball. I mean I never thought of growing up in the sence that I always wanted to feel the same way I always remembered feeling. Lou was quoted as being 'the luckiest guy on earth.' Mabey he hung out with me too much cause I consider myself to be the most absurdly fortunate guy to have slid into the 20th century safe."

OCTOBER SERIES

Both are tall and slender
And she has very good breasts.
He looks like a medical student
Whom she believes, nodding,
When he explains everything about
How the playoffs go:
Two games in Kansas City, then three in New York,
And how it's very important for the Yanks
To get at least a split: AWAY—
And two would be super, of course—
Because of the home advantage after.
She is almost as tall as he is but his arm is
Around her comfortably, as they walk ahead,
And it is clear that he very much wants her
To understand how this goes,
The Phillies and Dodgers getting started tonight,
And it's clear too that she wants
Very much to get this straight,
Listening, and looking and looking at him
As if his face is the diamond.

I suppose you expected a pun like that
Or that you didn't expect a pun like that,
But they were so lovely on their way
What I wanted to make
Was a double-play metaphor,
The med to the beauty to me—
Not like that but tricky and elaborate, turn two,
And then around the horn.

JIM BROSNAN

HARDBALL, AUNT STEVE, AND THE WHITE SOX

I'd been going to big league games since I was five. My old dad thought it was educational. So did his sister Stephanie. They'd take me on Sundays whenever the Cubs were at home. One time, I got to the South Side to see the White Sox. Learned something every time out. Like a good player should.

"Born to play ball!"

That's what Old Dad said about me. Gave me a ball to play with when I was still in the crib. Only kid on the block who cut his teeth on a baseball stamped: OFFICIAL AMERICAN LEAGUE. WILLIAM HARRIDGE, PRESIDENT. My security blanket was an old sweatshirt. Sleeves cut off. Faded letters on the front:

NEW YORK YANKEES WORLD CHAMPIONS 1948

Old Dad was a big man with hairy hands, a gap-toothed smile, and a grand vision of the future. Mine, of course. His was shot already and he knew it. But he would make a big leaguer out of me if it killed me. Isn't that what a father's for? If he isn't good enough to make the big time by himself he makes his kid do it. It's an unquestionable part of the American Dream.

Aunt Stephanie was one of three sisters. Noisy middleaged virgins, they hung around my crib on visiting days, Sundays, and most holidays. Telling each other who I looked like. Pretending I was God's gift to the family. Pestering me till I screamed for Momma.

I liked Aunt Stephanie, though. A real horse. Long face, wet nose, heavy chest. She'd clop through the house, wheezing with asthma, laughing a lot. Too loud. Momma'd try to hush her up soon as she walked into the house.

"Please, Steve, don't wake him!"

Ha! I could hear her half a block away, slamming out of her old car, snorting up the steps, plowing through the doorway.

"I'm here," she'd yell. "Anybody there?"

Give an old girl like that a smile and look out! She's all over you. And clumsy! Picked me up out of the crib one day like I was a rosin bag. Those horny hands grabbed me right in the belly. Buried my nose in her collar, puffing up a cloud of scent sweet as chloroform. Enough to make a guy gag. Or think to crap his pants. And, at that age, thinking was doing, so she'd drop me soon as she could.

Old Dad liked Aunt Stephanie too. He thought she was the only girl in the whole family who made any sense. Aunt Stephanie was a baseball fan. The others, Momma included, didn't know from nothing.

"Steve," Old Dad would say, "you shoulda been a

Andy Nelson

boy. You got the makin's. Big hands. Long legs. Strong
back. Too bad!''

Aunt Stephanie looked more like a boy than a girl.
Tall and ugly. Not ugly-ugly. Pretty ugly. Like a catcher.

Momma liked Aunt Stephanie just a little bit. As
though she was afraid of her but didn't want to admit it.
Old Dad would give Aunt Stephanie a big hug whenever
she came around. Just kidding, of course. But Momma
would giggle and Aunt Stephanie would yell: ''Hands off,
Hardball!''

Old Dad would roar at that. ''Hardball'' had been
his nickname when he was a semipro shortstop. Nobody
but his old buddies and Aunt Stephanie could call him
''Hardball.'' Momma never dared.

Old Dad and his sister looked at life the same way,
mostly. Aunt Stephanie had only two things she worried
about. Baseball and The Church. Nothing else mattered.
You wanted to talk about something else? Forget it. Fans
and fanatics. That's all she had time for.

Old Dad was a churchgoer. Typical son of an Irish
Catholic. Devout, but in-and-out. He'd go to the cathe-
dral and play the religion game for an hour every Sunday.
Then he'd walk out and around the rest of the week and
you couldn't tell him from a Baptist or a Jew. Only, you
better not compare him with a Jew. He hated them worse
than he did Jackie Robinson.

''Nigger ballplayers!'' he'd yell when he read me the
box scores at Sunday breakfast. ''Takin' over the game!''

Aunt Stephanie would shush him. Bang him on the
head with Our Sunday Visitor. Put her hands over my
ears and whinny, loud enough to wake the neighborhood.

"That's not Christian, Patrick O'Toole! The Good Lord made us all to be brothers!"

"Would you marry one, Steve?" Old Dad would say, pushing her off me. "Huh? Would ya? Huh?"

That was Old Dad. Strong sense of family ties.

The thought of marrying anybody made Aunt Stephanie blush. She wanted to love everybody like a brother. Even Negroes. Especially if they were in Uganda. She laid out money every Sunday morning to help black men build good homes in the jungle.

When I was five we'd go to the ballpark after church. Me, Old Dad, and Aunt Stephanie. They even took me once when I was just a baby. Carried me through the grandstand in one of those car-beds. Set it up in the aisle behind home plate. (Old Dad always bought good seats.)

They gave me my bottle. Bought beer for themselves. When the game started, they ignored me and concentrated on the pitcher. That was okay. Plenty of folks around me to wave at. In the seventh-inning stretch the TV people played their camera on me from the broadcasting booth. So I stretched. Just as if I knew the game.

The Cubs had a bad ball club that season. So the TV announcer made a joke about "You can see this team is building for the future." The sportscaster wasn't any too good that year either.

The Cubs got worse instead of better in the next few seasons. Old Dad and Aunt Stephanie and me, we were about the only fans who showed up, regularly, every Sunday afternoon. We'd go to Mass, go to the park, eat hot dogs, and see the Cubs.

Well, Old Dad would boo. And I would boo. But Aunt Stephanie would pray, because it was Sunday and the Cubs needed all the help they could get.

"God damn!" Old Dad would say when a Cub booted the ball.

"God help us!" Aunt Stephanie would say as another unearned run scored.

"Jesus Christ!" Old Dad would groan when a pop fly fell between three Cub fielders.

"Jesus, Mary, and Joseph!" Aunt Stephanie would cry. "I swear that ball should have been caught!"

I knew more profane ejaculations at the age of five than most players know when they get to the big leagues. Learning the language helped me learn the game too. After one season in a box seat with Old Dad and my aunt I had grasped the first rule for being a big league fan: "If you can't say something good about a professional, say something bad about him."

That's life in the big time. It's black or white. It's win or lose. You're right or you're wrong. Any five-year-old should be able to understand that.

Since we lived in Chicago, we didn't always have to watch the Cubs. When they were on the road, we could take the elevated and go to the South Side to see the Sox, who were in the other league.

It wasn't the same, though. It just wasn't. Not that the Sox were such a bad team. They just weren't *our* team. If you're going to be a Real Fan, you have to pick a team and stay with it. No matter what your team does. That's the law, and if you follow the law you can boo your brains out at the park if you like.

Old Dad was a Real Fan. He said he wouldn't go to

the Sox park if you paid him. He said they didn't even know how to play the game in the other league.

He'd watch the Sox on television, though. He'd turn the sound down and watch the picture while he was listening to the Cubs' radio broadcast from St. Louis, or Pittsburgh, or wherever the Cubs were playing. Momma said he was confusing me. How was I ever going to learn anything just watching pictures with no one to tell me what was going on.

Silly Momma! I knew what was going on! The pitcher threw the ball and tried to get the batter out. And when he got three outs, a funny black bear would make a pitch about beer. Who needed an announcer? All baseball games sound the same on TV anyway.

Aunt Stephanie didn't care who was playing. She said she'd go anywhere to see a game. She said a fan owed it to himself to see as many games as possible. Old Dad's attitude toward the Sox was ridiculous.

"You're nuts, Hardball!" she'd say, laughing so he wouldn't be hurt.

"At least I ain't a traitor!" he'd yell. "What kind of Catholic Cub fan are you? Rootin' for the Sox! Would you root for the Baptists? Would you root for Cassius Clay?"

"I think I'll take the kid to the South Side with me one of these days," said Aunt Stephanie, grabbing me round the neck like she was saving my life.

"Over my dead body!" cried Old Dad.

"He's never been on an El train, has he?" she asked. Shrewd old girl! She had me sold, right there.

"What's that got to do with it?" asked my puzzled pa.

Heck, getting to Sox park is half the fun of seeing them play.

Old Dad went up to Milwaukee one July weekend when I was seven. His annual reunion with old semipro teammates. They'd get together to cut up all the active big leaguers. Tell each other how much better baseball was in the good old days.

Aunt Stephanie saw her chance. She showed up that Sunday just as though the Cubs were in town.

"Wanna go see the Sox play, Polly?" she asked Momma.

That was good for a laugh. Momma snorted, lady-like. I just froze, halfway through my pitching motion. Which wasn't easy since I had been winding up to throw a rolled-up sock at the living-room wall. That's what Old Dad wanted me to do. He liked to say: "When this kid grows up, he's gonna fire the old pea right through a brick wall!"

Old Dad had his eye on the future. Would have made a great scout.

Aunt Stephanie called time when I fired my high, hard one into the fireplace, and she took me to Sox park. Put a Sox cap on my head. Carried my finger-mitt in her own hand. Pushed me onto the El train. Giggled to herself all the way to the South Side. She was having so much fun she nearly ruined my own good time.

Aunt Stephanie claimed I got lost that first time down there in Sox country. Ha! How can a guy get lost in a ballpark? You gotta keep your eye on the ball all the time. Right? And if the guy you're with has his eye on the ball, too, why you're with him. Right? Even if you're in another part of the grandstand. Heck, I'd been going to ballparks all my life. Lost! I didn't miss a thing all day.

What happened was, I got picked up. You take any blond, blue-eyed boy of seven, with a tendency to look tearful, and you got a surefire wolf-bait for every born, bachelor-uncle, baseball fan. Anytime I wanted a taffy apple or peanut brittle bar, a couple of goodies I wasn't supposed to have, I just dripped a tear on my downy cheek and a flock of would-be mothers in long pants fought to feed me.

Not that my tears came easily. I was no instant crybaby. It always helped if the team I was rooting for happened to be kicking the game away. Then I'd drip true sorrow from at least one eye. And if I could get back by the refreshment stands, it was picnic-time with the nearest Good Samaritan.

Anyway, Aunt Stephanie got all screwed up in her scorecard trying to record exactly what happened in a doubleplay that started with a fly ball and ended up in a rundown between third base and home. You know. The kind that gets scored 9-2-5-2-5-2-1, with the pitcher covering the plate for the tag after the catcher and third baseman finish playing pass over the base runner's head while the right fielder runs all the way into the infield to be sure he gets an official assist.

So, while Aunt Stephanie was scribbling and figuring and erasing, I sneaked down the ramp to look for the little boys' room. At least that was my excuse if I couldn't catch the eye of a guy with a heart of gold and some ready cash.

Sure enough, the first refreshment stand I come to, a little guy with an unpressed coat and mismatched pants is waiting his turn for coffee. I run up next to him, bawling, then whip around in a circle a couple of times like I'm looking for somebody. Then I shriek, sliding away with a whisper, swiping at my nose. Gets 'em every time.

He gives me the soft con about "everything's gonna be all right" and "don't worry" and "how about a Coke" and soon I'm chomping on a caramel-covered Jonathan straight from a Yakima, Washington, orchard. As usual the little old guy just stands there admiring my appetite instead of chasing down an usher and reporting that he's found a lost boy. (That's the way they announce it in the grandstand: "A little boy has been found lost" and everybody laughs except the dumb mother who's missing a kid.)

What happened this time at Sox park was, Aunt Stephanie comes hurtling down the ramp from the stands, looking like a steeple-chaser. She spies me, pulls up, paws the apple core from my hand, and turns on my sugar daddy like she's gonna nip his nose.

"Dirty old man!" she yells. "Keep your hands to yourself!"

Poor slob. Here he'd been a good sport and what did it get him!

"Beat it before I call a cop," says Aunt Stephanie.

A cop yet! She could have pinched the little guy's head off all by herself. He shuffles off, though, so she turns to me, tenderly tugs my ear, and whispers at full volume: "Gotta go to the little boys' room, huh?"

I just nodded because my tongue was busy cleaning the sweet caramel off my upper lip. Aunt Stephanie drags me through the WOMEN door, pops me into one of those stables, and yells: "Hurry up! We're hitting! Listen!"

The crowd is yelling in the grandstand, stamping their feet, making enough noise above us to scare the pee out of a guy who wants to get back in time to see the action.

"It's stuck! I yell, faking a loud sob. I was in just as much of a hurry as she was but I had my own little game to play.

Every time Aunt Stephanie took me into the WOMEN I got my zipper stuck, or pretended to, and she had to come help me. She couldn't stand it. Made her mad. Face got red. Hands shook. She'd get to mumbling and fumbling and by the time we left the place she'd forget all about the taffy apple, or caramel corn, or whatever I'd managed to mooch.

We hustle back in time to see a Sox player slide hard into the catcher and knock him down. When the catcher flips backward, he knocks the plate umpire down too. That's the way they play the game in the other league.

Anyway, the Sox player is called out. Never had a chance. Catcher had the plate blocked. All he had to do is hang on to the ball. That's how the ump saw it. Me too. And maybe Aunt Stephanie. She didn't say.

Twenty thousand fans start to boo. Half of 'em curse the umpire. A couple hundred start throwing things. Seat cushions, scorecards, popcorn boxes. Things like that. No beer bottles. No hard stuff. It's against the rules in the big leagues.

Aunt Stephanie's yelling too. While we'd been gone, somebody kicked over her beer cup. Somebody snatched her scorecard. Somebody dropped a wad of bubble gum on her seat. Now it's stuck to her skirt. She picks at it with one hand, points north with the other, and cries: "You were right, Hardball!"

We never went to the South Side again.

COBB
ON
ROSE

What makes Ty Cobb such a fascinating figure in baseball history is the fact that he was not just one of the game's greatest players; he was also perhaps its most complex personality. That being the case, it is interesting to consider how Cobb would have reacted to Pete Rose and his surpassing Cobb's record for career hits. In seeking answers to such questions, *Spitball* consulted the world's foremost authority on Ty Cobb, Charles C. Alexander, author of the definitive Cobb biography (*Ty Cobb,* Oxford University Press, 1984). The following conversation took place Saturday, September 7, 1985, in Cincinnati, Ohio, with Pete Rose only three hits away from breaking Ty Cobb's record. We are grateful for Mr. Alexander's generous cooperation.

SB: Did Cobb play as long as he did with the idea of putting his hit record out of reach?

CA: No. He held forty-three records when he retired. And though he set most of them in 1927 and '28, his last two years, the main reason he played was that he simply didn't want to give up playing. In '27 he had something to prove also, with the Cobb–Speaker scandal. Dutch Leonard had accused Cobb and Speaker of fixing a game and betting on it back in 1919. He felt that his honesty and integrity had been called into question, and he felt

PETE ROSE 14 4192

CINCINNATI 1B

Darryl Lankford

that he had to play to vindicate himself. As you may recall, "Vindication" is the title I gave to the chapter of my book which covered those years.

Of course, the big record for Cobb was surpassing Honus Wagner's career hit total (of 3430) in 1923. The Detroit writers and *The Sporting News* took note of it, but the attention the accomplishment received was not anything like the sensation when Ruth was setting his home-run records. As Cobb set his records, it was simply observed that he had surpassed this player or that player. You have to understand that it was a much less statistics-oriented era. No monumental levels of performance such as the ones we have become accustomed to judging players by had been established yet.

When Cobb got his 4,000th hit, he read about it in the afternoon papers, but there was no big deal made about it. There was simply a different attitude then toward records and what it meant to break a record.

SB: Did Cobb consider his hit total his greatest record? Was he more proud of it than any of his other totals or accomplishments?

CA: To my knowledge Cobb never singled out any performance record as being the one he was most proud of. He was most proud of having received all but three of the votes cast when he was nearly unanimously elected to the Hall of Fame in 1936. He was very proud of that.

I suspect that if he were alive today Cobb would regard his .367 lifetime batting average as his unbreakable record.

He felt too that considering the present trend in base

running nobody would ever steal as many bases again as he had in 1915 [96]. Cobb was unhappy with the changes that had occurred in the game; as early as '23 he was a strong critic of the new power baseball, the home run, the big-inning game . . . the decline of stealing, the hit-and-run, etc., etc.

When I was a kid, this was said all the time: "Nobody will steal more than ninety-six bases." That was when players like George Case were leading the league with low totals, say thirty or forty. So you see, at that time Cobb's total looked insurmountable.

In a 1952 piece he wrote for *Life,* Cobb had taken baseball to task . . . saying that nobody was stealing bases anymore, and so on and so on. Well, *Life* hired Rogers Hornsby to write a rebuttal, and Hornsby wrote that if Cobb were playing in 1952 he would never steal ninety-six bases because he wouldn't try, because he wouldn't get that many opportunities to run. In that context . . . of power baseball with the emphasis on home runs and big innings, it seemed impossible for anybody to exceed ninety-six stolen bases in a season. Ironically, Maury Wills broke that record by stealing 104 the year after Cobb died.

SB: Of course, Cobb never saw Rose play, but if he had, what would his opinion of him have been?

CA: Cobb would have liked Rose; would have admired the way he plays; he would see in Rose the way he played the game.

Cobb's attitude would be: "Here's a guy I'd pay to get into the park to see play."

However, without question Cobb would see himself as being far superior overall to Rose. As he was. Waite Hoyt felt the same way.

Cobb would see Rose as a throwback to the old players. The attributes Rose is famous for . . . his hustle, dedication, staying in shape, playing a full season, practicing self-denial, those things made up Cobb's approach to the game. As a matter of fact, Rose has been hurt and out of the lineup a lot less than Cobb was. Rose's breaking Cobb's record is as much as anything else a tribute to durability. Rose has had more chances to accumulate hits than Cobb, but we should admire Rose for being able to be healthy for so long. For a forty-four-year-old man Rose has remained in terrific shape.

SB: Somebody, Cobb's son, I believe, has suggested that an asterisk be put by Rose's hit total because of his greater number of plate appearances. You feel then that that's unnecessary?

CA: Yes, I think so. It doesn't make any sense. It would have made as much sense to put an asterisk by Cobb's name when he broke Wagner's record. Cobb got more plate appearances than Wagner because he managed to stay in better shape than Wagner, and Rose has managed to stay in better shape than Cobb.

Cobb had no sympathy for players who didn't keep themselves in top condition. He criticized Joe DiMaggio for getting out of shape in the off-season; he thought DiMaggio never reached his full potential because he didn't keep himself in the best condition year round.

And Cobb could never understand how Ruth could do what he did on the field and then do what he did off the field. Ruth broke all the rules, and his ignoring all the training precepts that Cobb lived by certainly contributed to Cobb's animus for him. It angered Cobb that it was so easy for Ruth and so hard for himself.

SB: How would Cobb feel about all the hoopla made over Rose's pursuit of his career hit record? Would Cobb feel less appreciated?

CA: Undoubtedly, he would find all the ballyhoo and public buildup tiresome. He would feel it was being overdone; after all people hadn't made a fuss over him.

If he were alive today, Cobb definitely wouldn't like to see the record broken. As you know, he didn't exactly fit the mold of the good sportsman.

Cobb could cite you chapter and verse the advantages that Rose, in playing under modern conditions, had over him . . . just as Rose could do over Cobb. It's interesting, the players from each generation or era are able to make such a strong case for their own greatness.

Cobb, for instance, would have thirty-five to forty extra hits a year on artificial turf. And then he played under the disadvantages of the dead ball, heavy shoes, soggy fields, heavy uniforms . . . you can go on and on. You can make a ledger filling up this side and that and go on and on with the contrasts between Cobb's and Rose's day and, of course, you could come out on either side.

SB: Interestingly, one of the many similarities between the two men has to do with their ability to make money. Rose has certainly capitalized on all the attention, and Cobb knew how to make a buck too.

CA: Yes, that's true. At twenty-two and twenty-three

Cobb was already making good investments. By the time he retired at age forty-one, he was a millionaire when a million dollars was a lot of money. In fact, that was part of Cobb's problem after baseball; he had no money problems in retirement, and he could do whatever he wanted to.

He lost money on a couple of minor league ball clubs he bought stock in; as far as I know they were the only losing investments he made.

One little-known fact about Cobb is that in 1929 he had a chance to buy the Cincinnati Reds. He made a bid, evidently a low one, and he wouldn't raise it because he was leery by then of putting money into ball clubs, and so he lost the club.

Moneymaking for Cobb was part of his propensity of bettering himself: he would study something until he mastered it to improve himself.

SB: Like Rose today Cobb was a player-manager. Could Cobb have played for Pete Rose, the manager?

CA: No; Cobb could not play for any present-day managers. Cobb always played on his own; he had his own style. Hughie Jennings, the Detroit manager, always let Cobb do what he wanted. At bat Cobb gave his own signals. He would step out of the batter's box and flash the hit-and-run, for instance. When Cobb was involved, the signs did not come from Jennings in the third-base coaching box.

Today managers insist on maintaining absolute control over every aspect of the game. The other day Whitey Herzog put in three different pitchers to pitch to three consecutive batters. Of course, at the same time Rose was using three straight pinch hitters. Cobb also engaged in overmanaging.

In his last two years with Connie Mack he was a different base runner from earlier in his career. In his prime Cobb ran wild; he did what he wanted to on the bases. You couldn't stop him. If Cobb thought he could make the next base, Hughie Jennings couldn't stop him. Cobb would run right through a manager's stop sign.

No manager today would put up with that kind of independence from a maverick like Cobb. As a player Cobb would have trouble with Rose or Whitey Herzog, but Rose and Cobb would like each other.

sb: What do you think about Rose's naming his son "Tyler," supposedly as a tribute to Cobb?

ca: The name is definitely a manifestation of Rose's obsession with Cobb. The name is a compromise; Rose wanted to use "Tyrus," but his wife said no.

Rose has always been very aware of Cobb and his accomplishments, but I don't think he has studied him. I know he has a copy of my book, and I know that his agent has read it; but I doubt that he has.

sb: Can you think of one word that describes what Cobb and Rose have in common?

ca: Not one, but I can think of two words: "total commitment." More than any other player with the ability to do it, Rose has had the commitment and the will to do as good as he can do and to keep himself in shape to be able to do it.

Both men were self-made stars. They made themselves into great players. And I'd say that that was the most admirable quality in both men. Many other players with as much or more ability weren't willing to pay the price.

Cobb started with mediocre talents. He didn't hit all that well in the minors at first—neither did Rose—and Cobb had no particular talent for the outfield. Cobb made more errors than any other outfielder in history; of course, he had more chances to.

Rose couldn't run; he has played various positions; the reason for his versatility is that he was not particularly good at any position. He's never been indispensable at any position, like, say, Joe Morgan, who was irreplaceable at second for the '75–'76 Reds teams.

There have been greater talents around than Cobb and Rose. The way to account for these guys is what's between the eyes; with them it's what's upstairs that really counts.

AROUND A BALD CYPRESS TREE

Mildred and Andy grew up and still live in a small town. Ottowa marks the edge of a coastal plain twenty-five miles south of the lakeshore. Every night Mildred and Andy walk across the town square, around a Bald Cypress tree in the southwest corner, and back home again. About once a week they stop by the bookstore after it is closed and peer through the windows.

Mildred worries about children and whether the Beatles will ever regroup, cats, and who engineered the assassination of Salvador Allende. Andy thinks about red beans, the Houston Astros, and old Lefty Frizzell tunes.

This particular Sunday in late September the five-thirty sun warmed their faces headed toward the Cypress tree.

"I read in *Rolling Stone* that George Harrison sent letters to the others suggesting a last memorial concert series. A trip around the world, sort of," Mildred said.

"That's annual," Andy answered, and nothing more was said of it that night.

The evening came on cooler than recently and Andy sat wrapped in a blanket, committed to leaving the furnace system shut down until November 1. Mildred never seemed bothered by extreme temperatures. She read an old collection of Cleanth Brooks essays. Andy was listening to a Hank Williams, Jr., tape and reading the *Sporting News*.

"I'm afraid the Astros have fallen out of the pennant race," he said.

"That's annual," Mildred answered, and nothing more was said of it that night.

BOB FELLER

Signed off his dad's Van Meter (IA) farm by the Cleveland Indians for a bonus of $1 and a baseball, Bob enjoyed a spectacular rookie season in 1936 at the age of 17; striking out 15 in his first start and 17 on Sept. 13 vs. the Philadelphia Athletics to tie the major league record.

Perhaps the game's fastest pitcher ever, "Rapid Robert" went on to pitch 3 no-hitters and a record 12 one-hitters. He also won 20 or more games six times (266 total), led the AL in strikeouts six times (2581 total), won the Triple Crown in 1940, and was elected to the Hall of Fame in 1962.

Jeff Vankanegan

GERALD BRENNAN

THE BALLPARK IN BALTIMORE

The ballpark in Baltimore is an anomaly in the world of baseball. Baltimore has always been the backwater of the circuit. Ask the man in the street, and he will simply deny the ballpark's existence. "There's no baseball in Baltimore . . . why have a ballpark?" He is startled, taken aback, flabbergasted to learn that indeed baseball is still played here. "Well then," he challenges, "where's the ballpark?" You tell him. "Why, I thought they razed that neighborhood for an expressway back in '62."

The ballpark in Baltimore is shaded from the sun and open to the sky. A street, pitched, potholed, and repitched, cuts through the summer haze and skirts the entrance. A lone billboard tiptoes across the way trying to peek onto the field. RUN ON ACME TIRES.

At the gate to the ballpark in Baltimore, inside a high-ceilinged cinder-block shack, sits the main ticket office. The window is framed by rusty girders, painted once then forgotten. The Ticket Vendor is a gnarled old man with close-cropped bristly gray hair and a rumpled threadbare cardigan half unbuttoned. All day long he shoots the breeze with two concessionaires who work the stand across the cement walkway. The three men have worked the park as long as anyone can remember.

The ballpark in Baltimore offers new patrons a special discount. Five dollars buys a book of forty coupons. Each coupon gets you into a game for fifty cents. The Ticket Vendor's memory isn't very good, though. He sells the ticket books to anyone. In fact, he usually just gives them away. "It's a great way to see the big leaguers in action," he says.

The Hawker at the ballpark in Baltimore keeps constant watch for customers, rocking his eyes swiftly back and forth, calling every potential sale by the same name. "Hey, Looie, c'mon over here." The Stocker unendingly replenishes souvenirs that never seem to sell. He is usually bent over, rifling through one cardboard box or another, searching for some particularly elusive item. Between selection and display the Stocker invariably involves himself in the ongoing conversation. Sometimes it takes him hours to put up a single article.

The three men who work the ballpark in Baltimore talk all day but never discuss a game once it has ended. Indeed, they rarely talk baseball at all. When the crowd boos, screams, murmurs, or moans, they know immediately who legged out a double or snatched a fly off the grasstops or eyeballed a third strike. They pause momentarily and listen. Any opinions are communicated in the twitch of a brow, the wave of a palm, or at most a few grunts.

To reach your seat at the ballpark in Baltimore you have to walk across the thick grass in right field, step carefully over the freshly chalked foul line, and climb seven rickety wood steps into the stands.

Partial inventory of the ballpark in Baltimore: mitts, balls, spikes, mound, rake, hose, cage, coach, masks, flag, slab, tarp, stubs, box, bucket, bullpen, alley, stirrups, on-deck circle, bags, fence, bench, fungo, plate, towels, shower, sweat, dirt, sky.

The air is dense, refractory at the ballpark in Baltimore. During the long stretch days of August the glare of the sun shimmers everything to a standstill. Occasional optical distortions cause the appearance of multiple balls, batters, fielders, etc. Games fork off to various conclusions depending on one's inclinations. (A vicious rising liner is sliced toward left. Trapped in the sweltering heat sweating off the earth, the ball shivers for an instant, then splits into two separate entities. The shortstop spins to his gloveside, pirouettes high into the air, feels his pocket explode. In the same motion he whips the ball sidearm to first, beating the runner back to the bag by an eyelash. Another ball sails over the leaping infielder's head and is grabbed near the line on the second bounce. The second baseman swipes a tag at the batter sliding headlong. The umpire signals safe; the second baseman curses audibly. The batter rises quickly, quietly, and asks time to brush off the front of his uniform. His hit rolls all the way to the fence in deepest left-center. He rounds second without hesitation and is in standing at third, a run scoring ahead of him.) Longtime fans accept, even savor, the fluctuous nature of reality at the park.

Play stops at the ballpark in Baltimore whenever a ball is hit into the stands. Five minutes or more can pass while the horsehide is chased down. Older fans drift in its direction casually, exchanging pleasantries along the way. Youngsters run the ball down frenetically and dodge others who try to snatch it away. Players wait out the delays pragmatically: they examine their spikes, pound glove leather, or just park a hand on a hip. The elderly return the ball with an awkward underhand toss. Young ball-bearers parade the stands, flaunting their booty before lobbing it back into play. It is a game with adolescents at the park to bluff a fielder in with the ball, then throw it as far as they can over his head.

Umpires dislike the ballpark in Baltimore. Anyone—a jangled manager, a green-eared waterboy or Fred Doak's grannie—is apt to charge onto the field, arguing calls with the men in blue, invoking sandlot regulations, waving thumb-worn rule books that jibe with their own conclusions. They throw up their hands, huff and puff, beseech heaven, point significantly at balls, bats, bases, anything close at hand, then wink sidelong to nearby spectators. Disagreements eventually move to the baselines, where another ump or a fan can act as mediator. Often the umpire is then called upon to settle technical arguments among fans in the seats. Play continues on the diamond in the meantime unabated.

The ballpark in Baltimore has a stream that wanders down the left-field line. It is populated with smooth boulders and schools of nearly microscopic fish. The brook meanders to and fro, somehow never crossing onto the field of play, until it finally disappears under the stands near the home dugout. Shade trees scattered throughout left and center add to the rustic flavor.

At the ballpark in Baltimore games are played in the sunlight, and all players, even the home team, wear gray flannels. Sometimes the outfielders lean against the shade trees.

The Ticket Vendor is still jawboning when you leave the ballpark in Baltimore. The concessionaires are busy dealing wares, like the pennants from the championship team they had here some years back. The date, stitched in bright yellow thread, may be apocryphal. No one remembers for sure. There is, however, great nostalgia for the colorful flags, even if they do hearken to an event that never occurred.

The air is cooler outside the ballpark in Baltimore. The crowd scatters in a hundred directions. A bus pulls up; its headlights blind momentarily. A discarded newspaper describes the day's pitching matchup, and the day and the game recede faster than the bus can make the long ride home.

JAN BRODT

MICKEY LOLICH, AFTER THE FACT

I came to the shop.
It seemed appropriate
During the series week.
The walls lined with pictures,
The series trophy
Displayed on center stage,
There only when he is.

Same body, little paunch,
Still looks young, slightly gray,
He's been out of the game
Only five long years.
I wished him well
With the Hall of Fame.
He hoped for a good long look.

I complained we'd never had
A good lefty starter
Since they traded him.
He laughed safely,
Seemed quietly pleased.

133

Some fans at the counter
Talked of Northup's hit,
Did Flood just lose it?
He said he'd seen the films
So many times.
"Way over his head."
I'd wondered and was glad.

"Must put my baby to bed,"
He said, gently picked it up.
He gave me a moment
To feel the trophy.
He was on his way
To the stadium,
High in the stands
Among the minions.

I bought two dozen doughnuts,
Some blueberry muffins,
Good as mother used to make.
I kept a box top
Among my souvenirs.
I hear he wanted
The Padres to win,
Lest we forget.

BILL HOWARD

THE CHARLIE PEPPER LETTERS

Tallahassee, November 4, 1980

Dear Mr. Corrado:

You will have to excuse the inexcusable delay in my answering your letter of Aug. 20. Since my retirement I am afraid that I have become lazy and a great procrastinator. After all those years of working under pressure to meet some paper or other's deadline, it is a real pleasure to spend the day puttering around the house doing practically nothing at all or watching one of the teams over at the University. I am a big Seminole fan these days.

Your project on the Reds teams of '39 and '40 sounds exciting; that was a great ball club, and it's about time that somebody has thought to do a book about them.

I will be happy to help you in any way I can, as long as you stick to what happened on the field. In my day we figured what a fella did on his own time after the game was over was his own business and not something to embarrass him with by making headlines out of—as the practice seems to be today.

I suppose there's very few people still at the *Enquirer* who

Darryl Lankford

know me as more than just a name payroll sends a check to every month. It's nice to be remembered though, and I thank you for the kind words about my work in Cincinnati.

Sincerely,

Charlie Pepper

Tallahassee, December 15, 1980

Dear Mr. Corrado:

I am glad that your work on the book is going so well. I apologize for the tardiness of this response, but preparations for the holidays—especially Christmas card writing—have kept me very busy.

You are right about the Reds catching: it was the best in the league. All you ever hear about anymore is how great Johnny Bench is. Everybody except old-timers like me seems to have forgotten how good Ernie Lombardi was. Bench is a great one, that's for sure, but he never won a batting title like Ernie did. (Actually Ernie won two: one for the Reds and one for Brooklyn.) Ol' Schnozz could really handle the bat, and if he'd had any speed whatsoever he'd have batted a good twenty-five or thirty points higher every year. The infielders played Lombardi so deep—knowing they had extra time to get the throw over to first base—that it was like batting against seven outfielders.

The fellas on the team really looked up to Lom too. He was a real leader on that club, not a phony rah-rah type, but somebody all the guys respected and looked to in the clutch. Ernie took a lot of friendly kidding about his nose and his slowness afoot, but there wasn't a more loved man on the team.

Harry Danning of the Giants was a terrific catcher in those days too, and, of course, Gabby Hartnett is in the Hall, though he was nearing the end in '39 and '40, but I'd still give the nod to Lombardi. The Reds backup catching, as you said, was also "unusually" good.

Well, that's about it. Hope these notes help with the book.

Sincerely,

Charlie Pepper

Tallahassee, February 8, 1981

Dear Mr. Corrado:

Your theory about the dissension on the Oakland A's and Yankees teams of the seventies being the catalyst that led to their championships is interesting, but I would guess that they won in spite of all the bickering, not because of it. There's no substitute for talent in the big leagues.

Concerning the '39–'40 Reds, there was no dissension that I was aware of—besides the usual (and natural, even inevitable) and minor friction that develops whenever a group of twenty-five men are thrown together and have to live together for a stretch of eight or nine months.

Good luck with the book.

Sincerely,

Charlie

Tallahassee, February 20, 1981

Dear Mr. Corrado:

In my opinion Bill McKechnie was a great manager, absolutely deserving of his niche in Cooperstown. Winning pennants with three different organizations (a major league record, by the way) is hardly a matter of "being in the right place at the right time." He had baseball smarts, and he knew how to handle a ball club. He got the most out of all his ballplayers, and they played as hard as Ty Cobbs trying to win for him. The fellas on that club loved Bill McKechnie, and he treated them like sons. You don't see that kind of bond much in professional sports anymore.

As you probably know, Mr. McKechnie was a very religious man (sometimes called "Deacon Bill"). He was a patient, kind, understanding man whose word was nevertheless always law.

I'm not sure I know what you seem to be hinting at in asking whether I think he made "any serious errors"; over a 154 (or 162) game season every manager makes some moves that backfire, but I don't think anybody could have done a better job with that team than Bill McKechnie.

Sincerely,

Charlie

Tallahassee, February 27, 1981

Dear Mr. Corrado:

No, I don't mind if you call. However, please don't phone in the evening as my wife and I retire rather early.

Charlie

Tallahassee, March 4, 1981

Dear Mr. Corrado:

As I told you on the phone yesterday, I am not eager to discuss Willard Hershberger. His suicide is still a disturbing memory, and as I told you from the beginning, I think a ballplayer's personal life is off limits for a writer—even after he (the ballplayer) has passed on. Let me add that in my day I believe we had more respect for people and their dignity than writers do today. We certainly never viewed a tragedy or another man's misfortunes or mistakes as an opportunity to advance our own careers, and I think we handled Hershberger's death properly; that is, as delicately as possible.

I would not like to see Willard's suicide sensationalized even now—after so many years have passed by. However, if you give me your word that you will treat the matter respectfully and if you let me see your manuscript before you send it off to the publisher, I will discuss it with you—to a point.

Sincerely,

Charlie

———————

Tallahassee, March 10, 1981

Dear Mr. Corrado:

Yes, you have the basic facts concerning the "Hershberger case," as you put it, correct. One reason I've always been reluctant to discuss the matter is that people can never seem to keep the facts straight. Something always gets distorted or fabricated. Even several days after Willard had killed himself and we had already put down the basic circumstances in the *Enquirer* as simply and as accurately as we could, there were wild rumors going around.

One rumor had it that Willard had killed himself over a New York show girl who had spurned him, and another had it that a beautiful female fan had murdered him because he jilted her. Both rumors, as you know, were equally ridiculous. I guess they both had something to do with Hershy's (his nickname, by the way) reputation as a ladies man. Years later I heard a man old enough to know better say that Willard "blew his brains out because he had dropped a third strike that cost the Reds the Series". When people don't even take the trouble to get a story like that straight, they don't have much business going around gabbing about it.

There's really not much I can add to what you've learned by reading the old *Enquirer*s. We put down what we thought propriety and decency allowed and what was sufficient to inform the public, and we left it at that. Although finding the body in the bathroom gave me a tremendous shock and made an impression on me that I have never been able to forget, I see no reason to bring up in your book the graphic details of the deed.

Sincerely,

Charlie

_____

Tallahassee, March 20, 1981

Dear Mr. Corrado:

You've raised a very interesting question which is also a quite sensitive one. And it is a question that I am certain everyone who had daily contact with Hershberger then has asked himself a million times since.

I suppose the reason no one saw it coming was that the suicide was such an exaggerated response to what Willard was feeling or experiencing that there was no way for anyone to conceive of such a thing really happening. The fellas knew Willard was depressed about the game he supposedly lost for the team in New York—he felt like he had called the wrong pitch—but nobody blamed him for Danning's home run. Hell, Danning was an All-Star player, and though he was a cousin of Bucky's, no pitcher gets his patsies out *all* the time. Nobody even dreamed of putting any blame on Hershy for that—not even Bucky who took the loss (in the ninth, after leading 4–1, I think) very hard. (I will never forget Bucky just standing out on the mound, staring up into the stands with a blank look on his face, all alone while the N.Y. fans are going crazy.)

And then you have to remember that the team was in a race at the time. The boys had almost been caught the year before in '39 by the Cardinals, and they were definitely feeling the pressure in August of 1940. To make things worse, Lombardi was out with an injury (that's why Willard was getting so much playing time), and the heat that summer was unbelievable—I don't remember a hotter summer in my life. All these things kept everybody's mind occupied and a bit on edge, and I guess Willard's depression just looked like what everybody else was going through, maybe just a little worse.

Besides all this, Willard was basically a loner. He was friendly and usually pretty cheerful, and he was popular with the team and the fans, especially with the ladies, but he was not very gregarious.

After it happened, everybody, of course, felt just terrible, even sick about it. But nobody could be blamed for anything. There was just no way to see it coming.

I hope these comments help you with this footnote in the story of the '39–'40 Reds. Please remember your promise to give me a chance to approve the Hershberger segment of your manuscript before you submit it.

Sincerely,

Charlie

Tallahassee, April 25, 1981

Dear Mr. Corrado:

Although I don't remember the remark and can't find it in my notes, if you read it in the *Enquirer,* then I will vouch for it as I had editorial control over our coverage of the tragedy and did most of the writing myself anyway.

I realize how Hershberger's saying "My father committed suicide and I will too" must look from this distance; but as I said in my previous letter, there was just no way to foresee him taking the action he did. Even if anybody on the club did hear Hershberger make such a statement, they would surely not have taken it seriously—nor should they have been expected to since ballplayers say things every day they don't mean.

Sincerely,

Charlie

Tallahassee, May 8, 1981

Dear Mr. Corrado:

Yes, of course, Mr. McKechnie knew that Willard was upset about the loss in New York, and he became very concerned when three or four days later in Boston Willard was still worrying himself about that game. But I don't think even Mr. McKechnie realized how upset the boy really was until the night before it happened.

We lost the opener in the series with the Bees, and then something unusual happened in the second game. Willard was catching, and somebody bunted the ball in an obvious sacrifice situation right out in front of the plate, and Hershberger didn't make a move to field it. Naturally, everybody was stunned, especially Mr. McKechnie, who called time and ran out onto the field to ask Hershberger if anything was wrong. Willard said, "You bet there is. We'll talk about it after the game." There wasn't much for Mr. McKechnie to do but leave it at that, so he went on back to the dugout. That night they got together over dinner and had a long talk. That is when Willard told Mr. McKechnie he was contemplating suicide. Nobody knows what else was exactly said during their meeting, but they talked well into the night, later in Willard's room at the hotel. The next morning, however, I had breakfast with Willard and he said that Mr. McKechnie had given him "a dandy pep talk" and that he felt much better, that he was no longer depressed.

So there again it was just totally unexpected. I'm sure that Mr. McKechnie was still concerned about Willard, but his spirits did seem to be improved, and as manager, Mr. McKechnie had twenty-four other ballplayers to worry about too—not to mention the Cardinals, the Giants, and the Dodgers.

I have tried so many times since then to remember every

detail of that morning to recall whether I was convinced by Willard's words and behavior at breakfast. I must have been because I don't remember being suspicious that anything was amiss.

Later that day at the park when Mr. McKechnie told me what the situation was, I did become alarmed. As you know, Willard never left the hotel that morning to go to the ballpark. When Gabe Paul, the club's traveling secretary, called him to ask why he wasn't at the park for batting practice, Willard said he was sick. Mr. McKechnie asked him to get dressed and just come to the park to give the boys some moral support. Willard said he would, but he still hadn't shown up by the time the first game was over, so Mr. McKechnie asked me to go over to the hotel and check on him.

The maid let me into Willard's room. When we found the room empty and the bathroom door closed, I knew then for certain that something terrible had happened. But, curiously, I never suspected even for a second that I would find Willard Hershberger on the other side of that door with his throat cut.

There really is nothing else that I can tell you about Hershberger. Surely you know enough to cover this tragic episode in your book, and I trust that it will receive a relatively minor treatment in the book overall. It is always better to concentrate on the positive, and there are many happy, fortunate things about that ball club for you to accentuate.

I am afraid that this correspondence is beginning to wear me out, and to be truthful I am glad that we have gotten to the end of it. I will not take long in editing the part of your manuscript about Hershberger.

Sincerely,

Charlie

_____

Tallahassee, May 19, 1981

Dear Mr. Corrado:

Yes, I am afraid that there is nothing to do but take the motivation for Willard Hershberger's suicide "at face value" as you put it. I am not qualified to psychoanalyze anybody, and I refuse to try. I would even balk at applying the word "abnormal," which is a psychiatric term. Besides, this is the sort of prying into a person's privacy that I've told you before I don't believe in. I will say that as far as I'm concerned Willard Hershberger was as normal a human being as I ever met. He was an excellent backup to Lombardi—even though his arm was a little weak—and he had a great career ahead of him. It was just a tremendous shame that he didn't live to achieve it.

So, again, if there was anything beyond his feelings that he was bringing the ball club down that caused his suicide, it will have to remain a mystery now.

Please send the manuscript so that we can tie things up. My wife and I are leaving town on vacation soon, but I will be sure to return it to you before we go.

Sincerely,

Charlie

Tallahassee, May 27, 1981

Dear Mr. Corrado:

This is my final letter to you. I have not been happy with the direction in which your questions have been leading, and I resent the insinuations contained in your last letter. I have been honest with you from the beginning—which is more than I think can be said for you in your dealings with me.

No, I see nothing "callous or avaricious" in the team's ability to win the pennant and World Series after the tragedy. Aren't you aware that they voted a full share of their take in the Series to Hershberger's mother? And I told you before that there were many wild rumors surrounding the death of Hershberger, and that business about my finding and destroying "a suicide note" is one of the most irresponsible that ever got circulated.

I now doubt that you will ever send the manuscript to me to approve of, and so I wash my hands of any responsibility for the contents of your book. I insist that you leave my name out of the book's credits, and I urge you not to slander the good name of Willard Hershberger or anybody else connected with his unfortunate and sad demise by speculating on things that you don't know anything about and which are destined to remain a mystery forever.

Sincerely,

Charlie Pepper

THE SPITBALL INTERVIEW:
JIM BROSNAN

From 1956 to 1963 Jim Brosnan was a relief pitcher in the major leagues, throwing his slider (his "out" pitch) for the Cubs, the Cardinals, the Reds, and finally the White Sox. His best years were with Cincinnati (the city in which he was born and where he grew up), for whom he went 29–13 over four years. In 1961 as the mainstay of the Reds' bullpen, he posted a 10–4 record (with a 3.04 ERA and sixteen saves) in helping Cincinnati win its first pennant since 1940. Lifetime Brosnan was 55–47.

Nicknamed "The Professor" because of his voracious reading and his fascination with words and language, Brosnan—at the urging of *Time* magazine reporter Robert Boyle—made literary history by becoming the first ballplayer to himself write without the aid of a "professional" writer an "inside" account of a major league baseball season. The resulting work, the diary of the 1959 season he spent with the St. Louis Cardinals and the Cincinnati Reds called *The Long Season,* became an instant and controversial hit and remains today one of the best baseball books ever written.

In 1961, "Broz" wrote a sequel worthy of *The Long*

Season, a diary about the Reds' championship year called *Pennant Race.* The two books not only paved the way for subsequent "inside" accounts such as Jim Bouton's *Ball Four* and Sparky Lyle's *The Bronx Zoo,* but they also launched Brosnan's career off the field as a radio commentator, columnist, and freelance writer.

1985 is the twenty-fifth anniversary of the publication of *The Long Season,* and *Spitball* is proud to celebrate the event by presenting "The *Spitball* Interview" with Jim Brosnan.

SB: Jim, how did you get into pro baseball?

JB: Cubs scout Tony Lucadello signed me to a contract in the fall of 1946, soon after the American Legion National Tournament at Charleston, S.C. I pitched for the Robert E. Bentley Post team in Cincinnati, which included Jim Frey and Don Zimmer, Cub manager and coach at present. The Cubs paid me a bonus of $2,500; my first contract called for $125 per month. That was a small bonus, but it was actually more than I made in my first three years as a pro!

SB: You spent eight years in the minors before breaking in with the Cubs. Very few players are given that much time anymore to get to the majors. Would you say that reaching the majors faster, today's players appreciate it less?

JB: Minor league apprenticeships were typically five years or more in my time. And I spent two years in the army during that apprenticeship. Too long, of course, but it took me a long time to learn my craft. Today, with a vastly reduced minor league system, I'd never have gotten a chance in the big leagues. A quick rise to the top doesn't guarantee success; in fact, it is much more difficult to learn at the top. So I tend to feel sorry for players who don't get enough fundamental training before they reach the majors.

sb: Did the players, either the Cardinals or the Reds, know you were writing *The Long Season?*

jb: No, I did not tell anyone that I was writing *TLS,* and so far as I remember the fact was not disclosed by my publisher.

sb: How did you preserve the material of the book, especially all the conversations which read as if they are verbatim? Did you take notes somehow or just rely on your memory?

jb: My memory used to be very good. And I was selective in what I chose to retain for notes that I transcribed as soon as possible after an unusually worthwhile dialogue. Since I was constantly reading or writing or working puzzles, it was possible to make notes even in the clubhouse, although I seldom did so.

sb: I assume most people were flattered to be in the book. Did anybody resent your portrayals of them?

jb: Contrary to your assumption, few people were flattered to be in the book. My wife's uncle, maybe. Jim Murray. Don and Gwen Studt, close personal friends. But not players, and certainly not coaches and managers. Solly Hemus was still incensed in 1962 when he coached for the Mets; from the third-base box he made several

Blair Gibeau

profane comments on my past, present, and future, on and off the mound where I was easily retiring his batters.

sb: Did you get any hostile "you violated the trust of the locker room" reactions?

jb: Well, the Milwaukee Braves visiting clubhouse man posted an extra large copy of the message that appears in many clubhouses: "What you see here, what you say here, when you leave here, let it stay here." I took it as a not-too-subtle gesture, but perhaps I was too sensitive.

sb: Can you remember any specific reactions to the book by players?

jb: The reactions of most players to my book ran the gamut from indifferent to antipathetic. Few said they really liked it; some players' wives said they enjoyed it. Larry Jackson of the Cardinals told Ken Boyer that I had never pitched well enough to write a book! And Gino Cimoli, a Card outfielder, was heard to say that he'd punch me in the nose the next time he saw me. (Actually, my roomie, Howie Nunn, got us together in the Rendezvous bar in Cincinnati where we downed a few beers instead.)

Frank Sullivan, a Red Sox pitcher, told me that if all I knew about pitching was in my books, then I should be ashamed . . . and maybe drummed out of the pitchers' union. But he did admit that the book was funny and that I should be proud of my sense of humor. And because I liked martinis, he invited me to go sailing with him in the Bahamas. I didn't go. He and catcher Sammy White had to be rescued by the coast guard when they did make the trip.

To be perfectly frank, writers—Peter DeVries, Rex Stout, Mark Harris, and others—liked the books more than ballplayers. I'm not sure what that says about the books, or the writers. But since my motivation was to see my name on my book in a local library, I'm happy I did it.

SB: How were the reviews of *TLS?* Were any particularly hostile or vitriolic?

JB: The reviews of *TLS* were nearly all favorable, but the only one that counted then and is still treasured was that of Red Smith. He was a writer whose work I admired very much; to have him say nice things about my writing was most pleasing. (A New York scribe named Rosenthal took me to task for my grammar! I wiped my ass with his review along with that of Joe Reichler, who said I was a "traitor to baseball.")

SB: Were you ever discouraged—either directly or indirectly—by any of your managers or by the baseball hierarchy from writing?

JB: My writing about baseball was discouraged by every general manager I played for in the majors. And Fred Hutchinson, my manager at Cincinnati, asked me directly not to write about the 1961 World Series, in which we were ignominiously crushed by the Yankees. (I did do a post-Series piece for *Sports Illustrated* with Hutch's concurrence.)

There was a clause in the standard big league contract that gave the club authority to forbid publication by the player without prior permission. Bill DeWitt of the Reds pointed out that during one contract negotiation, but when I pointed out that writing was an avocation, he didn't press the issue. Instead, he traded me to the White Sox!

SB: Well, what happened then? You had a good year for the Sox [3–8, but fourteen saves and a 3.13 ERA], but that was it. Were you released, injured, blackballed, or what?

JB: The first words out of Sox GM Ed Short when he met me were: "You're not going to be able to write here, either." During our contract talks the following spring of 1964 he was adamant about it. And because I had sold two pieces during the winter, I was equally stubborn. So he finally released me outright. So, yes, I had my problems with management about my writing.

I never thought that I was blackballed as such after my release. Thirty-four years old, losing some of the snap on my out-pitch, the slider; a reputation, undeserved, of being a troublemaker; lack of any aggressive attempts to get a job: these were the reasons why I stopped pitching when I did.

SB: You were an essential part of the Reds 1961 championship team. Was helping them win the pennant your biggest thrill?

JB: Getting the last out in the pennant clincher has to rank with the big thrills . . . I can tell they're thrilling by the horripilation.

SB: Was not making the NL All-Star team in 1961 your biggest disappointment?

JB: Like any other professional athlete, I had a lot of disappointments, which I quickly forgot and don't ever want to remember.

SB: Was the World Series anticlimactic after the tough race in 1961? Did the Reds suffer a letdown, or were the Yankees just that much better?

JB: The 1961 Yankees were the best team I've ever seen in baseball. It was a pleasure being on the same field, even if we didn't belong there.

SB: Did you have any sense of being a pioneer in writing *TLS* and *PR?*

JB: To the extent that my two books were the first "insider's accounts" actually written by a player himself, I suppose you could call me a pioneer. And to the extent that I am still the only player who wrote without the help of a professional biographer (and actually got a book published) I guess I'll be proud to be a pioneer!

SB: What's your opinion of *Ball Four?* And why do you think it took somebody that long (1970) to follow in your footsteps?

JB: *Ball Four* was a funny book. Len Schecter did a heck of a job combining his vitriol with Bouton's jokes. I've no idea why such a book wasn't published sooner.

SB: There aren't any risqué passages in *TLS* or *PR* (besides the very subtle account in *TLS* of Don Blasingame and Joe Cunningham's last night on the town in Japan). Does this purity represent judicious editing on your part or the realistic behavior of ballplayers from a more innocent era?

JB: My editor at Harper & Row vetoed *sex* and tried to put the kibosh on *martinis!* He didn't want to ruin the juvenile market, he said. I went along with the former, but poured more gin as the days and pages unfolded. My idea was to save *sex* for the novel. (Red Sox pitcher Frank Sullivan told me that if I didn't know any more about *sex* than I did about pitching I should forget about it.)

SB: Was the success of the two books a surprise to you?

JB: The success of *TLS* was a surprise to me and an even bigger surprise to Harper & Row, the publishers. *TLS* is now rated a "classic," that is, it will remain in stock at H&R. There have been six editions, three hardcover, three paperback. All have made money for the publishers, and my profits put my three kids through college.

SB: In your books you often describe homers that soared over scoreboards or bounced off them, and the bullpens where much of the talk took place were real places, not just states of mind. These references to the distinct old parks that used to be around the NL are very nostalgic today. What's your opinion of the modern look-alike all-purpose stadiums?

JB: From a technical viewpoint a pitcher would be

inclined to prefer the big, new, multipurpose stadia over the small, irregularly shaped parks of my time. I know I'd rather pitch in Riverfront than in Crosley Field. But as a fan—or a nonworking pitcher for that matter—I liked the old ballparks, built for baseball, conducive to higher scores and the sight of pitchers having nervous breakdowns on days the wind blows out.

SB: You mentioned in *TLS* that you feel the hitter has the advantage over the pitcher. Do you still feel that way?

JB: As a pitcher, I thought hitters had all the advantages; as a hitter, however, I thought pitchers had them. As a fan, I enjoy most a balance in the contest between pitcher and hitter.

SB: There is a lot of talk in both books about specific players' weaknesses and strengths, about how to pitch to individual batters. Do you think the average fan is oblivious to this part of the contest?

JB: Yes. Analyzing hitters' strengths and weaknesses is beyond the scope of the average fan. Figuring out how and why the pitcher is working the hitter is equally esoteric for the fan. I do think that TV analysts like Kubek and Palmer and some others are educating those fans who listen while they watch telecasts of games.

SB: In *TLS* you evince a high regard for Sal Maglie as a pitcher and a low regard for the usefulness of Cards coaches Johnny Keane and Howie Pollet. Ironically, it seems, ten years later in *Ball Four* Jim Bouton portrays Maglie, then the pitching coach for the Seattle Pilots, very unsympathetically as the epitome of a "fifth wheel." Is the job of major league coach inherently more of a titular position than anything else?

JB: Sal Maglie was the consummate pitcher who got more batters out with less natural stuff than anybody I can remember. I don't know what kind of coach he was; he may not have been able to communicate what he knew. Today's coaches, by and large, are selected for their ability to teach, and I think they are very helpful to young players.

SB: Nineteen fifty-nine was Elroy Face's big, even monumental, year (18–1). Why so little talk of him in *TLS?*

JB: Elroy Face was a heck of a competitor, but he wasn't as good copy as Quiz and Rollie Fingers, nor did he last as long as Wilhelm and Sutter. But then, he wasn't as good as Lindy McDaniel, and who ever hears of him anymore?

SB: You had some interesting, basically critical, things to say about the reporters covering the game in '59. Many players today too feel that the press is too often insensitive or unfair (usually in the name of "the public's right to know"). Would you agree with them? And what's your opinion of the "silent treatment" policy of players such as Steve Carlton and Dave Kingman?

JB: The press is a hell of a lot more critical of players than they used to be. My bitch then was that the writers seldom knew much about the game they criticized, and that still is the case today. What's more, the writers now are ordered to get "inside stuff" on their beat, and that too often translates into criticizing the personal habits of the players. Still, I think Carlton, Kingman, et al, are wrong when they refuse to help promote the game.

SB: The carping Harry Caray depicted in *TLS* bears little resemblance to the one we hear today on cable. Has he changed that much?

JB: Harry Caray is less critical than he used to be. Wittingly or not, he does contribute to the rah-rah atmosphere that permeates the electronic media that cover the Cubs.

SB: Are you still sore at the Cubs for trading you?

JB: No. I'm now a rooting fan!

SB: According to what you mention in *TLS* and *PR*, you seem to have pretty high-brow reading tastes.

JB: I've read as much low-brow and middle-brow as I have high-brow. My reading tastes are eclectic. I value Ross Thomas and Robert Parker as much as Mark Twain and Vladimir Nabokov. All I ask for is style and entertainment.

SB: Do you read many baseball books? If so, what are your favorites?

JB: Yes, I read all the baseball books sent to me for review or comment. That's still a bunch each year. Recent favorites include Kinsella's *Shoeless Joe* and Hay's *The Dixie Association*. My all time favorites are Harris' *Bang The Drum Slowly* and Kahn's *The Boys of Summer*.

SB: The style in *TLS* and *PR* might be described as highly metaphorical, playful, and sarcastic—even cynical at times. And certain devices, such as the use of very short sentences to summarize and conclude an entry in the diary, are a big part of it. Would you agree with this description?

JB: My writing style parallelled my conversational style of twenty-five years ago. I neither talk nor write like I used to. As to my writing techniques I'm happy to accept your analysis. My own recollection is that I'd fool around with different approaches and use the one that felt right. And since I'd read thousands of writers for pleasure, I had plenty of styles to steal from, even if the theft was subconscious.

SB: What is the status of the novel you have been working on?

JB: For twenty years Harper & Row has been waiting for my first novel. The editor who worked with me on *TLS* is now the top man in the house, and though he's rejected three attempts at said novel he still claims I can do it, and he retains the option to publish it. I doubt if it will be done.

SB: Do you ever see any old teammates or foes?

JB: I still see socially Moe Drabowsky, a former roommate, and Johnny Klippstein, a former teammate in the majors. And John Pyecha and Bob Zick, former teammates in the minor leagues.

And, in pursuit of my baseball assignments, I run into many friends and acquaintances who are managing, coaching, and working in various front offices.

SB: One of the achievements of *TLS* and *PR* is the perfectly accurate rendering of the major leaguer at work, "at the office." One gets a great sense of what ballplayers say, of how they talk, of what they do among themselves. Would you agree that this insight the books provide is one of their biggest appeals?

JB: If I succeeded in anything, it was a realistic portrait of what some pros did and said during a season. Both books had a good "voice," I think.

SB: At the end of *The Long Season* you express a sense of great weariness. Is the theme of the book that baseball, as many fans forget, is hard work?

JB: Baseball is not work. It is, as Sandy Koufax told me last week at Dodgertown, "something we do until we grow up."

TOM SHEEHAN

IN COLD FIELDS

They left us then,
we in our sneakers
and innocence
of those bright summer days,
to go away from us
with our big brothers,
left us lonely and miserable
on corners, in cold fields
with all the long-ball hitters gone,
the big sticks of the neighborhood,
and the big wood of the Majors,
and we cried in dark cells of home
for our brothers and bubble-gum heroes,
a community of family.

Oh, Eddie's brother not yet home
from someplace in World War II,
Zeke's brother who owned the soul
of every pitcher he ever caught,
a shortstop the Cards owned,
Spillane, I think, his name;

and in that great silence out there
Billy centerfield left his arm
in Kwajalein debris.

Oh, brotherless we played our game,
no deep outfield, no zing to pitch,
no speed, no power, loveless
without a big brother
to show the growing.

And then, not long after the Braves
rode that mighty crest,
our turn came,
and we left our brothers
on corners, in cold fields,
we long-ball hitters.

Blair Gibeau

Ernie Banks

OLD-TIMERS

I have tended bar in this part of California for almost forty years, and I have seen my share of strange doings, I can tell you that. This time of year, when baseball season is in full swing, always brings to mind an incident that took place right here in this establishment in the spring of 1938.

It was a Sunday afternoon. Being the new kid on the job, I had to work. Everyone else was at the ballpark. We had a good town team in those days, mostly miners playing on their day off. A lot of other towns had teams, too, and we had a lively little semipro league. Good ballplayers, some of those fellers were. The mining companies would sponsor the clubs, and the local merchants would get behind them, and it was all great fun. Sunday afternoons, if you were lucky, you went to the ballgames. Guess it's not that way anymore, is it?

On this particular Sunday, I had the tavern to myself. Well, not entirely, I suppose. Over in a corner booth, all curled up in his dusty clothes like a hound dog, an old drunk lay sleeping off Saturday night. He had wandered in that evening and never left. Nobody knew

164

the guy; he appeared to be just another drifter, which you used to see a lot in these parts when the mines were going good. Since he wasn't bothering anyone, we'd just let him stay where he was. Sunday, when I opened up, he was still out like a light. So I cleaned the pool table and polished glasses, punctuated by the drunk's wheezy breathing, and waited for the after-the-ballgame crowd to wander in.

It was not your typical game that day. Our team was playing a club from somewhere in Arizona, who were barnstorming these parts and challenging all the teams. This was not uncommon then. You'd have these teams, sometimes with ex–major leaguers on them, and it was a way for the ballplayers to make a living. To be sure, some serious money would get wagered on the outcome of a game. If your town had a good team, like we did, you had a civic duty to accept all challenges. And the line on these Arizona boys was that they were plenty tough, so there was an especially large interest in this particular contest.

All week long rumors had circulated about the Arizona team. The gist of them centered on their first baseman. It was said he was a former big-leaguer and he was no slouch. But the main thing was, he had to be at least fifty years old! Word had it he creaked like a wagon running the bases, but he could still swing the bat, and in the field he was an absolute magician. Reflexes like a cat, even at his age. Well, everyone speculated on just how well some feller in his fifties could play ball. Didn't hurt the betting action, either. And then, on Thursday, a salesman came in and said he had seen the Arizona boys playing a few weeks before up in Chico. He said the first baseman was something else. Said he frolicked like a young colt, and you couldn't put one past him in the field. Saw him work a perfect hit-and-run three times in the same game and also sock a pair of triples. And that was not all, the salesman said. After the game, the first baseman had taken on all comers at the pool hall, and nobody could whip him. After this story, you could cut the excitement in the air with a knife. It was going to be some game, for everyone but yours truly.

On the day of the game, which was scheduled to be a double header, I'm keeping an old drunk company in the tavern. But I paid particular attention to readying the pool table. Something inside me figured that I would see this first baseman from Arizona before the day was done.

Sure enough, around six o'clock, a trickle of fans came through the door. They reported that the games had been split. The Arizona team was good, but their first baseman was far and away the star. There was no doubt he had played in the big time. But funny thing, he'd cost them a sweep by making a bad error on a routine play in the second game. Let an easy ground ball go right through his legs, after spearing everything else hit within ten feet of him. More people came in with further reports. The first baseman sure could hit for an old-timer. Suddenly, our own team poured into the bar, and with them was the main topic of all the conversations.

He was a big man and still looked trim, but the way the flesh hung on his face, I could tell he liked to drink more than he liked to eat. A good bartender can spot that right away. But he had a merry twinkle in his eyes and a thick head of red hair, and our boys seemed taken by him. They swept him up to the rail, and soon I was so busy drawing beer that I could barely keep up with the chatter. Mostly they talked about the games, and how it was too bad he had made that big error in the second tilt. And the first baseman said, "Boys, it won't be the last time I muff one. And besides, you didn't want us to leave with all your money, did you?" That brought a big laugh and drinks all around. They called the first baseman Harold and he bought his share of the rounds.

○ ○ ○

After a while, Harold said, "Have we got any pool sharks in the house?"

Well, that caused a stir, and soon the action shifted to the field of green felt. From time to time, I looked over and I could see that Harold was indeed a wizard with the cue. He made those balls hop to his command. Normally you wouldn't want to play a feller like that, but a few of the boys fancied themselves experts and Harold had some extra pocket money in no time. But he had such a winning personality, cracking jokes and keeping up a steady stream of patter, that no one got sore. Everyone was charmed by him and awed by his ability. A sportsman indoors and out, or so it seemed at the time.

Along about closing time, only Harold and two or three die-hards remained to carouse. Jimmy Fields, the surveyor, waved to me.

"Come over here and join us, Clem," he said. "You've worked hard enough today. Have a drink with us." So I did.

Harold was feeling no pain by now and his face glowed as red as his hair. But his eyes still twinkled and he had us all enthralled with his yarns.

"Yes, boys," he said, "I admit I did play awhile in the big leagues. But that was a long time ago. I don't expect anyone in the present company was even around." Guffaws around the table. "Well, I came up with the New York team in the American League, and 1906 was the year. The Yankees were known as the Highlanders then. A pretty good club and I was glad to be there."

"How did you hit 'em?" someone asked.

"Oh, not as well as I hit you boys today," Harold said, and that gave us another chuckle. "I must be reaching my peak now, eh? Couldn't hit the ball nearly as hard back then. We had the dead ball back in them days. Maybe you've heard of it. There wasn't a lot of home runs. We scratched for the hits and stole a lot of bases. And we faced some rugged pitching. Spitballs, shineballs, balls that were mashed flat on one side—they'd throw anything at us. Big Ed Walsh, he was a star then, he won forty games one year with a spitball that would warp your bat. We had a gentleman named Jack Chesbro on our club. He was almost through by then, but he could still load 'em up. A batter would hit one of his pitches down to you and you'd get a bath just trying to pick it up."

We all laughed at that, and Harold continued to drink and spin his tales about the great old ballplayers he had seen. Ty Cobb, Nap Lajoie, Eddie Collins, Home Run Baker—many of us had heard these names when we were kids. They had played long before the ballplayers we followed, like Jimmy Fox and Lou Gehrig. Harold had seen Babe Ruth pitch, for God's sake! It was hard to believe he was that old, fresh from an afternoon of running around the diamond. Joe Lyons told Harold he was putting us all on. Harold only said that Cy Young had pitched a no-hitter against his team and Young was forty one years old at the time!

The hour grew later. I looked up and saw the drunk stranger who had been asleep in the booth. Without our noticing, he had awakened from his long nap and had drifted over to our table. I guess he had been standing a few steps behind Harold's chair for a little while, silently taking in the stories. There was a growth of stubble on his chin, and his clothes were faded and rumpled. But I noticed his eyes were open and clear. He seemed to be listening intently.

"How long did you stay in the majors?" Sam Cotton asked Harold. Harold took a long slug of beer and sat back, gazing at a spot on the wall above Sam's head.

"Not that long," he said. "Never could get the knack of that pitching. I hung on as a utility player with a bunch of clubs until the war came. Never did get into more than a couple hundred games."

"Why don't you tell them the truth?" the drunk muttered.

We all looked at him and Harold swung around to face him.

"I know you," the drunk said, and pointed his finger at Harold. "I reckon I saw you play often enough. Why don't you tell these boys who you are? Haven't they bought your beer for you, and haven't you taken their money?"

Harold winked at us and said, "I think we'd better set our glasses down, boys. You can see how too much drinking affects the mind."

The drunk was not swayed by our laughter. He shuffled closer and looked Harold in the face.

"You haven't changed at all, have you?" he said. "All these years and you're still a liar. And I hear you made an error today and cost your team a win. Well, let me guess how it happened. You let an easy ground ball go through your legs. Or the shortstop made a routine throw and somehow you got your legs tangled up around the bag and didn't catch it and it looked like a wild throw. Or maybe the pitcher was covering and you made a little toss to him, but it was off just enough so he couldn't reach it. Which one was it? Or have you found a new way to lose a game?"

I started to my feet, but Harold motioned me to stay seated. The drunk man moved around to face the rest of us.

"This man," he said, "was without a doubt the best first baseman I ever saw, and there's many who will admit he's the best who ever played the position. Better even than George Sisler. But he won't deny that he liked to make a quick dollar, just as he's done tonight. Only he bet against his own team to lose, and always found a way to help his own cause if he could. You won't deny it, will you? No doubt you had a few side bets on the games today. Why even Christy Mathewson swore that this man deliberately threw ballgames, and who would doubt Matty? There never was a fairer man. Oh, they cleared this feller's name in a court of law, but everyone knew what he was doing. John J. McGraw finally sent him packing. Ran him out of the game in 1919, right in the middle of the season. It wasn't the war now, was it? Why, they say he even helped to set up the Black Sox scandal in the World Series that year. You won't deny it, will you? Because you know that I know."

The drunk coughed and cleared his throat. From Harold came not a single word of yea or nay. He appeared to be trying to size the drunk up, like he was some new pitcher with a baffling delivery.

"The shame of it all," the drunk continued, and his voice was calm and sad, "is that this man possessed a great talent. I said he was the best first baseman I ever saw. He made plays that words cannot do justice to. I've seen him field a squeeze bunt on the fly and tag the runner coming down from third. Ty Cobb himself admitted that he would never pull the ball against New York. That's a fact, boys. He was talking about this man right here—Mr. Harold Chase, otherwise known as 'Prince Hal.' "

"Who are you, old-timer?" Harold said.

"You don't know me, do you?" the drunk replied. "I'll grant you I'm a damn sight poorer than you may remember me. But I remember you. I remember how you couldn't hit a good fastball on your fists. And I remember you were a better hitter than you've told your friends here. Didn't you win the National League batting title in 1916 with a .336 average?"

"It was .339," Harold said.

"Excuse me," said the drunk. "It was, as you said, a long time ago. And yet you don't know me, do you? Look at my eyes. Don't you recall the way they studied you? You were only sixty feet away. Try to picture me with a younger, smoother face. Don't you recall how, even in your championship year, you couldn't hit a foul ball off me? Because I had a fastball in my prime. You weren't the only one who couldn't hit me, Chase. Don't you remember? Sixteen shutouts I threw the year you won your title. Three hundred and seventy-three games I won in my time and not a single one dishonestly. Your kind couldn't buy me off, could it?''

"Old Pete," Harold said softly. "Grover Cleveland Alexander.''

We stared at this drifter in the shabby clothes. Could this be the same man who fanned Lazzeri in the '26 World Series? It was said he had been a drinker, but there was no sign in his dusty appearance that a great star could have once inhabited this worn-out body. Even Harold still looked like an athlete. Hadn't he played a double header this very afternoon?

"You bum," Harold said evenly. "You drunken old fool. Look at you. What a mess you are. You look twenty years older than me, and I know you're a younger man. You had it all and you drank it away. I've heard about you, Pete. You're no stranger to a flophouse, are you? You're not above trading your Lazzeri story for a free shot, are you? And you stand in judgment of me. You embarrass me in front of my friends. And you want me to think I've sunk lower than you? Do I look it? I've got money in my pocket and friends to spend it on. I'm welcome wherever I go. People are glad to see me. I can still play ball, and no one cares about some ancient history. But they care about a sloppy drunk in their midst. Travel with me, Pete, and I'll show you which one of us they turn away at the door. Who of your old friends will have you now?''

The drunk straightened up and stood erect. He seemed uncomfortable in his clothes, as if he had suddenly noticed their battered condition for the first time. And then he reached inside a pocket and pulled out a long white envelope.

"I may have found hard times," he said, "but I have not been forgotten. Here is something you will never have, Prince Hal. All your lying and scheming and cheating and gambling will never win you what is inside this envelope. And you could have had this if you'd only been honest." From the envelope he took a letter and unfolded it. "I will read you all just the first sentence. It says, 'Dear Mr. Alexander, It is our great pleasure to inform you of your selection for the Baseball Hall of Fame in Cooperstown.' "

He paused. The room was so quiet you could hear the glasses soaking in the sink. Very carefully, he replaced it in his pocket. He came over to me and touched my arm.

"I want to thank you for your hospitality," he said. "I only planned to stop here for a drink after dinner, but obviously one drink is not enough for me. But I believe I'll be going now. The sun will be up soon. I was on my way to Los Angeles to find a train for the East. Some baseball people are expecting me there."

He shuffled to the door and never looked back as he went out. We watched him go and then turned to face one another. Only Harold kept his eyes on the door.

"That old son-of-a-gun," he said. "He always did have my number."